CREA

D&C
David and Charles

Foreword

Corrugated cardboard has become an indispensable creative material. In addition to the environmental benefits of using a recycled material, it exhibits many surprising aesthetic qualities.

Corrugated cardboard possesses a discreet elegance; its flexible, repetitive motifs and grooves give it a rhythm all of its own. Its texture is soft; its colours are warm and subtle.

It is an ideal material with which to invent shapes and create smooth effects: it is light and resistant and can easily be folded, curved, rolled and twisted.

This book aims to use corrugated cardboard to create a wealth of animals that are both imaginative and humorous.

Contents

· **Flexible cardboard** is corrugated cardboard with a groove. It has one smooth side and one corrugated side.

· **Black, kraft, white or blue micro cardboard** is a flexible corrugated cardboard with micro-fluting. It is flexible and available in various colours, with one smooth side and one corrugated side.

Materials and general techniques

All of the animals in this book are made using natural or coloured corrugated cardboard, sometimes decorated with coloured micro-fluted cardboard.

· **0.6 cardboard** is a type of rigid corrugated cardboard with double grooves. It is 6mm (1/4in) thick, with two smooth sides.

· **0.3 cardboard** is a type of rigid corrugated cardboard with a single groove. It is 3mm (1/8in) thick, with two smooth sides.

· **0.1 cardboard** is a rigid corrugated cardboard with a single groove. It is 1mm (1/16in) thick, with two smooth sides.

· **The essential materials:** a pencil, an eraser, a metal ruler, a set square, a pair of compasses, tracing paper, a small cutter, scissors, tweezers, a hole punch, a bradawl, a toothpick, vinyl adhesive, adhesive tape.

Flexible cardboard

0.3 or 0.1 cardboard

0.6 cardboard

Micro-fluted cardboard

Production

Simple techniques that will
enable you to make the animals
in this book.

Cutting

1 · **Drawings** must be traced
and reproduced directly
onto the cardboard with
a pencil before being cut
out. All geometrical shapes
mentioned (rectangles,
squares, circles, etc.) are
accompanied by their
dimensions.

· **Strips and sticks**
should always be traced
perpendicular to the grooves.

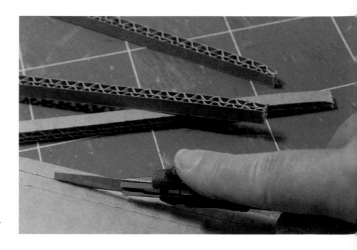

2

· **Cutting** should be done primarily with a cutter, using a metal ruler for straight lines. In order to obtain the cleanest possible cuts, the blade must be changed frequently.

· **0.6 cardboard** is used frequently and is also the most difficult to cut out, particularly when there are curved shapes involved. Start by gently scoring the layout with the cutter to create a track for the blade to follow. Then go over this track several times, scoring the cardboard until it is finally cut all the way through. During this process, the blade must be mostly taken out in order to give it greater flexibility, and kept perpendicular to the thickness of the cardboard so that it is not cut at an angle.

· **The smaller and more curved the shape**, the more essential this advice is. It is important not to place your other hand in the path of the blade, to avoid cutting yourself.

· **Flexible cardboard** should be cut on the corrugated side, keeping most of the cutter blade out.

· **Micro cardboard** can be cut with the cutter or with scissors.

Finishing

3 · **Vinyl glue** should be used so that it disappears when dry. To keep the assembly in place during drying, we recommend pinning it in position. To elevate a part, it is sufficient to glue a small piece of cardboard underneath as a wedge.

Cylinder

Spiral

Cone

Pieces of confetti

4 · **Decorations** are created for the majority of the animals using spirals, cones, cylinders and pieces of confetti.
· **A spiral** is made from a strip of flexible cardboard or micro rolled up tightly around a toothpick with the grooves facing outward. It only needs to be glued at the end.
· **A cone** is a spiral with the shape altered by pushing very gently in the centre. To fix this in place, coat the interior with glue.
· **A cylinder** is made by rolling up a rectangle of cardboard.
· **Pieces of confetti** are small circles cut out with the hole punch.

Useful decorative items

1

- **The mouse box:** Make a spiral with a 38 x 1cm (15 x ⅜in) strip of flexible cardboard.
- **Cut out** a 3 x 15cm (1¼ x 6in) rectangle from kraft micro and glue it around the spiral with the grooves facing out. Cut out a 4.5cm (1¾in) circle from kraft micro and glue it to the bottom of the box.
- **Make the lid** using the same method as for the box in a slightly larger size: the strip should be 39 x 0.5cm (15½ x ¼in) and the rectangle 1.5 x 16cm (⅝ x 6¼in). Attach a circle of kraft micro to the top.

Mouse and tortoise

Original boxes for storing milk teeth...

2

- **Head:** Draw and cut out two ears from kraft micro (A). Fold and glue them to the top of the lid.
- **Make a cone** for the snout from a 0.5 x 30cm (¼ x 12in) strip of kraft micro.
- **Make a small cone** for the nose with a strip of black micro. Glue the nose onto the snout, and glue the finished nose onto the lid.
- **Cut out and glue on** small strips of black micro for the whiskers, two rectangles of white micro for the teeth and two black pieces of confetti for the eyes.

3

- **The tortoise box and lid:** These are made based using the same method as the mouse box.

4

- **Head:** Cut out two 2.7 x 1.7cm (2 x 1½in) rectangles of 0.6 cardboard. Glue together then cut them at an angle (Diagram 1). Glue in place two pieces of black confetti for eyes, two black spots for nostrils and a fine black strip for the mouth. Glue the head onto the box (Diagram 2).

5

- **Legs and tail:** Draw and cut out two front legs (B), two back legs (C) and the tail (D) from 0.6 cardboard. Glue them onto the box (Diagram 3).

- **Draw and cut out** the scales in kraft micro and glue them onto the lid (Diagram 3).

Diagram 1

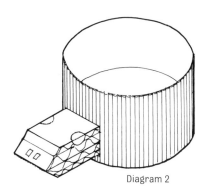

Diagram 2

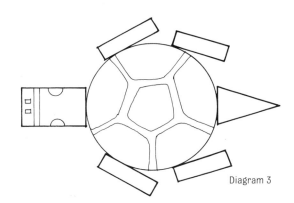

Diagram 3

Mouse and tortoise – actual size templates

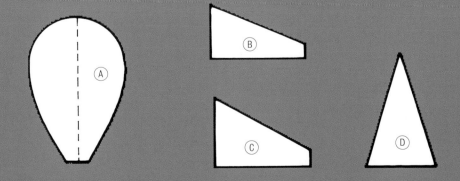

SUPPLIES

· 0.6 cardboard: 30 x 30cm (12 x 12in)

· 0.3 cardboard: 5 x 5cm (2 x 2in)

· Flexible cardboard: 18 x 8cm (7 x 3⅛in)

· Thick white paper: 11 x 3cm (4½ x 1¼in)

· Kraft micro: 5 x 5cm (2 x 2in)

· Black micro: 30 x 30cm (12 x 12in)

· White micro: 5 x 10cm (2 x 4in)

1 · **The body/box:** Cut out four rectangles of 0.6 cardboard; the base: 18 x 6cm (7 x 2¼in), two long sides: 18 x 4cm (7 x 1½in) and the short side: 6 x 4cm (2¼ x 1½in). Glue the short side and the long sides to the base.
· **Attach** two rectangles (four grooves) of flexible cardboard to the interior sides (Diagram 1).

Wolf

A decorative pencil box that will look great on any desk...

2 · **The back/lid:** Draw and cut the tail (A) twice out of black micro. Glue the two pieces together. Cut out and glue together two 18 x 5.8cm (7 x 2¼in) rectangles of black micro. Make a notch and glue the tail in the middle of one short side of the rectangles. Slot the lid into the space between the last two grooves (Diagram 2).
· **Seal** the box by gluing a rectangle of black micro onto the back of the body under the tail.

3 · **Legs:** Draw and cut out a pair of front legs (B) and a pair of rear legs (C) from 0.6 cardboard. Cover one side of each leg with black micro. Glue the four legs to the body, ensuring that the wolf balances (Diagram 3).

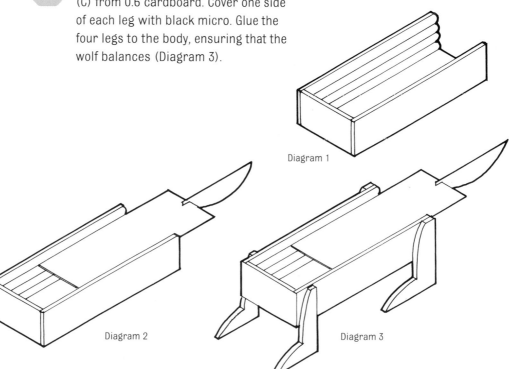

Diagram 1

Diagram 2

Diagram 3

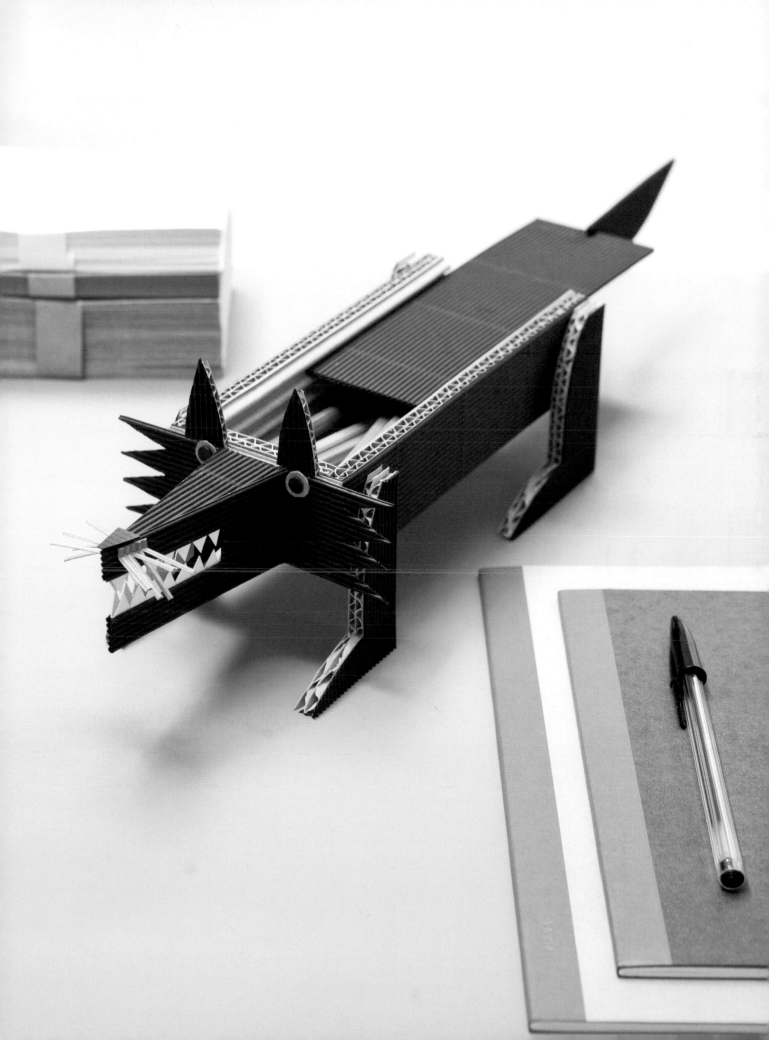

Wolf (continued)

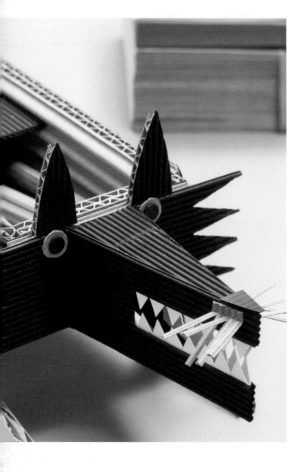

Head

4 · **Draw and cut out** the triangle (D) from 0.3 cardboard and cover it with black micro.
· **Draw and cut out** the head (E) from black micro. Cut out the central rectangle along the dotted lines to form the mouth. Use the cutter gently in order to be able to fold along the dotted lines; smooth side for the two sides, corrugated surface for the centre.
· **Draw and cut out** two corrugated strips of thick blank paper for the teeth (E). Use the cutter gently in the middle to make it possible to fold them. Glue the strips to the top and bottom of the mouth, smooth side.
· **Draw and cut out** the top of the head and ears (F) from 0.3 cardboard. Cover the ears with black micro.
· **Fold** the head (E), then glue it to the triangle (D) and the ears (F) (Diagram 4). Glue this entire section to the body (Diagram 5).
· **Glue** in place two circles of kraft micro with pieces of black confetti on top for the eyes, a small black triangle for the nose and two 1 x 2cm ($^3/_8$ x $^3/_4$in) rectangles of kraft micro with a 1.5cm ($^5/_8$in) fringe for the whiskers (Diagram 6).

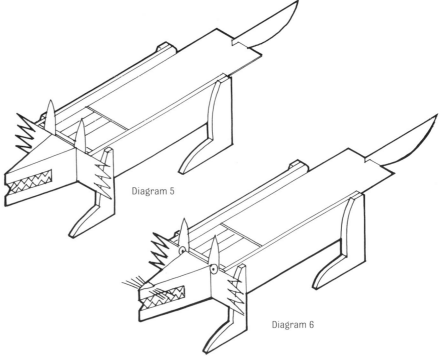

Diagram 5

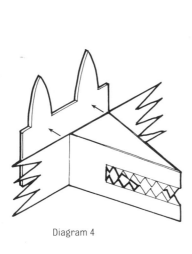

Diagram 4

Diagram 6

Wolf – actual size templates

SUPPLIES

· 0.6 cardboard: 30 x 30cm (12 x 12in)

· Flexible cardboard: 50 x 50cm
(20 x 20in)

· Kraft micro: 10 x 10cm (4 x 4in)

· Black micro: 10 x 10 (4 x 4in)

Body and head

1

· **The box:** Cut out two 10cm (4in) circles from
0.6 cardboard. Cut out a 34 x 9cm (13½ x 3½in) rectangle
from flexible cardboard and glue it around one of the
circles (Diagram 1).

· **The lid:** Draw an 8cm (2¾in) circle onto the second
circle. Cut out a 34 x 1.5cm (13½ x ⅝in) strip of flexible
cardboard and glue it around the circle, keeping the
circle you have drawn on the outside. Cut out a 25 x 1.5cm
(10 x ⅝in) strip from flexible cardboard and glue it onto
the outline of the circle (Diagram 2).

2

· **Head:** Make a spiral, 10cm
(4in) in diameter, with a 50
x 1.5cm (20 x ⅝in) strip of flexible
cardboard. Gently push the spiral
to obtain the volume needed for the
head. Coat the interior with glue.
· **Insert** the head into the lid and
glue it into place.

Cat

A container for sweets or sugar-lumps,
but do cats like sugar?

3

· **Ears:** Draw and cut out the ears (A) from kraft micro. Use fine strips of black micro
to make the edging around the ears. Glue them onto the cat's head.

· **Eyes:** Make two spirals with two 25 x 0.5cm (10 x ¼in) strips of kraft micro. Place
circles of black micro around these. Glue two pieces black of confetti in the middle
and then glue them onto the head.

· **Nose:** Draw and cut out the nose (B) from black micro. Glue it to the base of the
head, allowing it to extend slightly beyond the lid.

· **Mouth:** Cut out two rectangles from black micro: 4 x 0.7cm (2¾ x ¼in) and
3 x 0.3cm (1¼ x ⅛in). Glue them in a T shape to the back of the top of the box.

· **Whiskers:** Cut out six 4cm (2¾) long, thin strips from kraft micro. Glue them to
either side of the mouth.

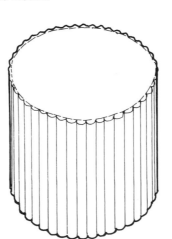

Diagram 1

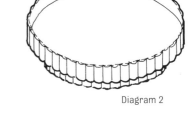

Diagram 2

Cat – actual size templates

Ⓐ

Ⓑ

SUPPLIES

· 0.3 cardboard: 36 x 36cm (14½ x 14¼in)
· 0.6 cardboard: 20 x 20cm (8 x 8in)
· Kraft micro: 10 x 10cm (4 x 4in)
· Black micro: 40 x 40cm (16 x 16in)

Body and head

1

· **Draw** and cut out two body profiles (A) from 0.3 cardboard.
· **Cut out and glue together** two 18 x 5.5cm (7 x 2¼in) rectangles (a), two 10 x 5.5cm (4 x 2¼in) rectangles (b) and two 4 x 5.5cm (2¾ x 2¼in) rectangles (c) from 0.6 cardboard.
· **Cut out** an 11 x 5.5cm (4½ x 2¼in) rectangle (d) and a 14 x 5.5cm (5½ x 2¼in) rectangle (e) from 0.6 cardboard.
· **Glue** the rectangles onto a profile (A) (Diagram 1).
· **Glue** the second profile onto the rectangles.

Hedgehog

A little pencil pot where the pencils blend into the prickles.

2

· **Draw and cut out** the base of the head (B) from 0.6 cardboard. Slightly fold the two sides of the head towards the interior (dotted lines). Glue the base between the two folded sides (Diagram 2).
· **Draw and cut out** the rounded part of the head (C) from kraft micro. Glue this rounded part to the curves of the head.

3

· **Cut out** two 1.5cm (⅝in) circles from kraft micro for the ears. Create notches in them and attach on either side of the head (Diagram 3).
· **Make** a cone for the nose with a 35 x 0.6cm (14 x ¼in) strip of black micro. Glue it to the bottom of the head.
· **Glue** on two pieces of black confetti for the eyes.

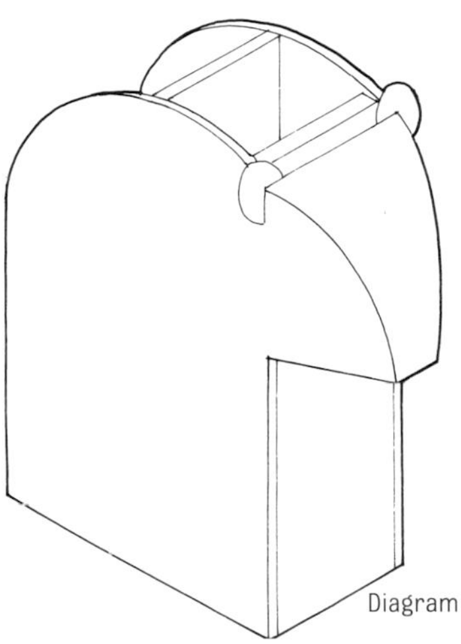

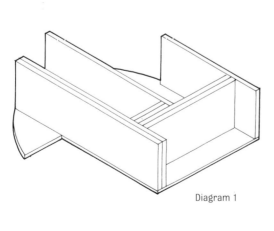

Diagram 1

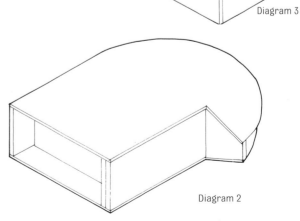

Diagram 3

Diagram 2

Hedgehog (continued)

Prickles and legs

4

· **Draw and glue** two sections (D) of black micro on each side of the hedgehog. Decorate the rear rectangle (d) with black micro (Diagram 4).
· **Cut out** six 6 x 4cm (2½ x 1¾in) rectangles from black micro (E). Create a fringe on them, cutting into each groove up to the dotted line. Fold, using a cutter gently along the dotted lines.
· **Glue** together and onto the head. Glue the four others onto the back of the hedgehog (Diagram 5).
· **Cut out** six 16 x 3cm (6½ x 1¼in) rectangles from black micro (F). Create a fringe and fold them as previously, then glue them onto the sides (Diagram 6).

5

· **Draw and cut out** ten body profiles (G) from 0.6 cardboard. Make two back legs by gluing three profiles together (Diagram 7), then two front legs by gluing them together twice in pairs. Glue the back legs to the front of the bottom of the body and the front legs 6cm (2½in) higher.

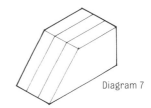

Diagram 7

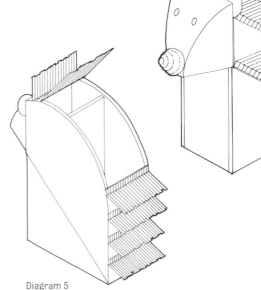

Diagram 6

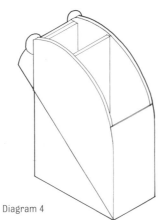

Diagram 4

Diagram 5

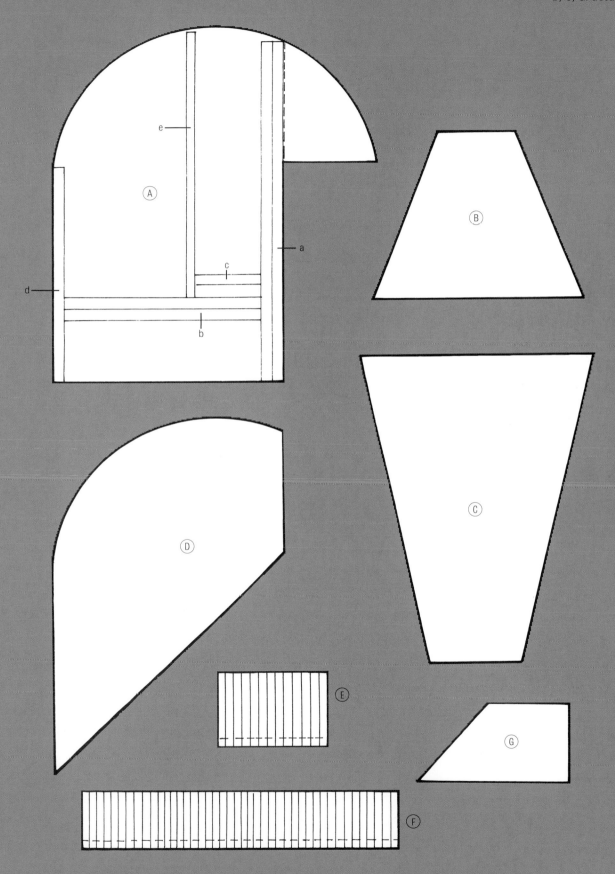

Hedgehog – A, D, E, F: enlarge x 200%,
B, C, G: actual size

The adult potholder

1

· **Draw and cut out** two body profiles (A) from 0.6 cardboard.
· **Cut out** three rectangles: 12 x 37.5cm (4¾ x 15in) (a), 12 x 23cm (4¾ x 9¼in) (b) and 12 x 22cm (4¾ x 8¾in) (c). Glue them to a body profile (Diagram 1), placing (b) 6cm (2¼in) from the bottom of the profile.
· **Seal** the body by gluing the second profile onto the rectangles.

Elephant

Enormously charming,
the adult can even hide a pot.

2

· **Draw and cut out** four profiles of back legs (B) from 0.6 cardboard. Glue them together in two pairs.
· **Draw and cut out** eight profiles of front legs (C) from 0.6 cardboard. Glue them together in two sets of four (Diagram 2).
· **Glue** legs to the body (Diagram 3).

3

· **Draw and cut out** two ears (D) from kraft micro. Fold these along the dotted lines and glue to either side of the head.

4

· **Draw and cut out** the trunk (E) from kraft micro. Glue it onto the rounded part of the head.

5

· **Draw and cut out** two tusks (G) from 0.6 cardboard and cover with white micro. Glue them to each side of the head.
· **Make** two spirals for the eyes from two 13 x 0.5cm (5¼ x ¼in) strips of black micro. Glue them onto the trunk, 8cm (3¼in) from the top of the head.

SUPPLIES

· 0.6 cardboard: 60 x 60cm (24 x 24in)
· Flexible cardboard: 50 x 20cm (20 x 8in)
· Kraft micro: 50 x 25cm (20 x 10in)
· White micro: 20 x 20cm (8 x 8in)
· Black micro: 20 x 20cm (8 x 8in)

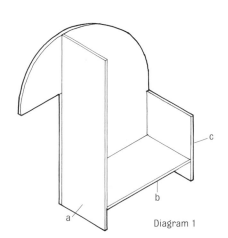

Diagram 1

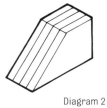

Diagram 2

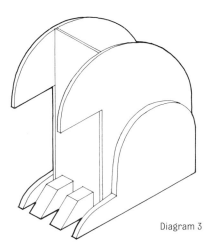

Diagram 3

Elephant (continued)

SUPPLIES

· 0.6 cardboard: 20 x 20cm (8 x 8in)
· 0.3 cardboard: 15 x 15cm (6 x 6in)
· Kraft micro: 12 x 12cm (4¾ x 4¾in)
· White micro: 2 x 2cm (¾ x ¾in)
· Black mini-beads

Baby elephant

1 **Draw and cut out** four body profiles (A) from 0.6 cardboard. Glue them together (Diagram 4).

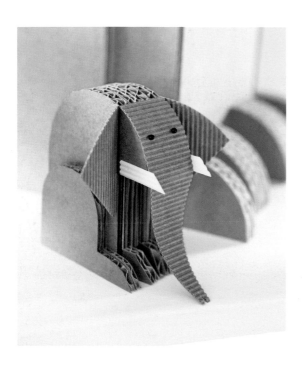

2 · **Draw and cut out** four back legs (B) from 0.3 cardboard. Glue them together in two pairs. Cut out two front legs (C) from 0.6 cardboard.
· **Glue** the four legs onto the body (Diagram 5).

3 · **Make** the ears and trunk following the same process as for the adult elephant (Steps 3 and 4), but making the trunk from flexible cardboard (Diagram 6).

4 · **Draw and cut out** two tusks (F) from white micro. Glue them onto each side of the head.
· **Glue** on two black mini-beads for the eyes.

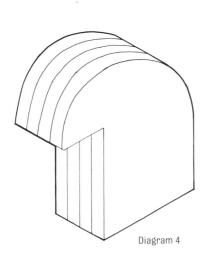

Diagram 4

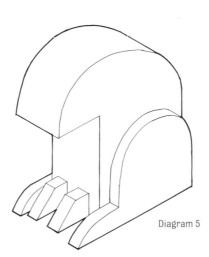

Diagram 5

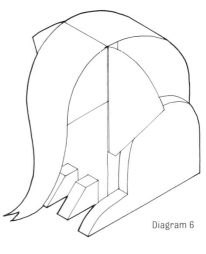

Diagram 6

Elephant – Adult: enlarge x 400% (except G, which is actual size)
Baby elephant – actual size

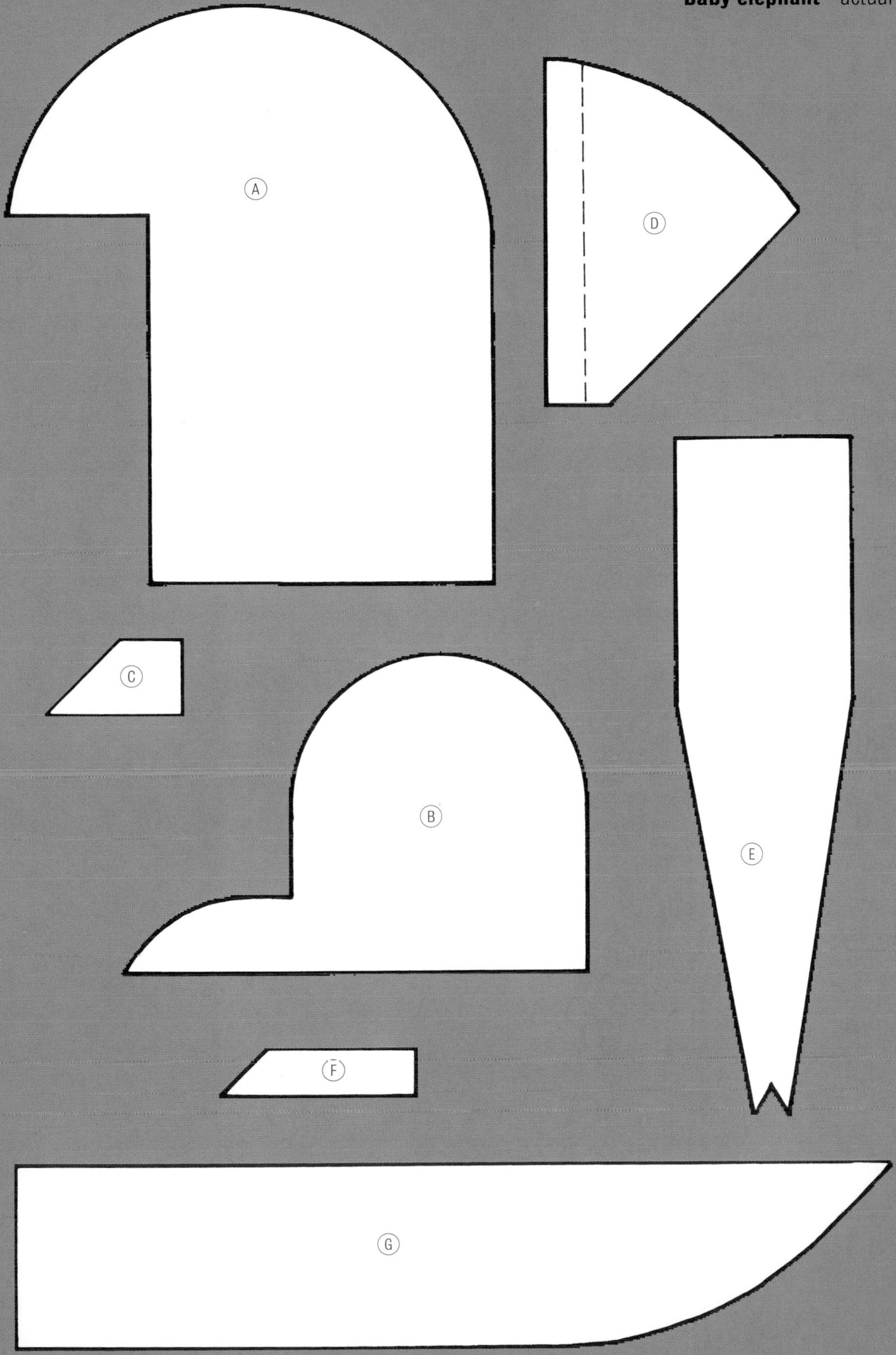

A

B

C

D

E

F

G

Clock

1 · **Cut out** four 22cm (8¾in) squares from 0.6 cardboard, with a rectangle cut out from each centre, should include one the shed on top of it (A). Glue the squares to each other, putting the square featuring the shed in third position (Diagram 1).

Noah's Ark

An enchanting clock to make before the rain starts coming down...

SUPPLIES

· **0.6 cardboard:** 60 x 60cm (24 x 24in)

· **0.3 cardboard:** 25 x 25cm (10 x 10in)

· **Kraft micro:** 22 x 22cm (8¾ x 8¾in)

· **White micro:** 10 x 10cm (4 x 4in)

· **Cardboard folders:** grey, brown and black

· **Tracing paper** 22 x 22cm (8¾ x 8¾in)

· **Clock mechanism and set of hands**

· **Punch**

2 · **The front:** Cut out a 22cm (8¾in) square from 0.3 cardboard. Punch an 8mm (³⁄₈in) circle in the centre. Cut out six 3.4 x 22cm (1³⁄₈ x 8¾in) strips of kraft micro, cut them to form the bricks (B) and glue them onto the front.

3 · **Dial:** Copy the dial template (C) onto tracing paper. Place the copy on the clock front and use the punch to mark the points on the dial. Glue a piece of confetti made from black or grey cardboard at each point of the dial.

4 · **Glue** the front to the bracket (Diagram 2). Insert the clock mechanism into the bracket and fix the hands to the front.

5 · **The shed:** Cover the roof and the top of the chimney with grey cardboard. Cut out and glue on a 3 x 2cm (1¼ x ¾in) rectangle from black cardboard for the door, and two 3 x 1cm (1¼ x ³⁄₈in) rectangles from kraft micro for the shutters.

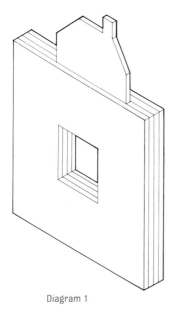

Diagram 1

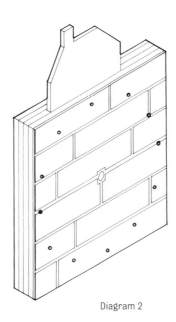

Diagram 2

Noah's Ark (continued)

Animals

7 · **Glue** the animal shapes to the back of the front piece all around the dial. The head of the cow is glued in front using a small piece of 0.3 cardboard; the same applies for the moose's antlers and the elephant's trunk. The monkey's leg is inserted into the slot on the dial.

6

· **Draw and cut out** the animal shapes, then decorate them:

The elephant (D) is made from grey cardboard: fold along the dotted line, decorate with two pieces of black confetti for the eyes and white micro for the tusks;

The snake (E) is made from grey cardboard, with black cardboard for the rings around the body and the tongue and black pieces of confetti for the eyes;

The moose (F) is made from brown cardboard, with kraft micro for the snout, black pieces of confetti for the eyes and half pieces of black confetti for the nostrils;

The donkey (G) is made from grey cardboard, with brown cardboard for the snout, black cardboard for the mouth and black confetti for the nostrils. The eye is made from a brown cardboard circle with a piece of black confetti for the pupil and the mane is made from black cardboard with a fringe;

The monkey (H) is made from brown cardboard, with pieces of kraft confetti for the ears, kraft micro for the muzzle and black pieces of confetti for thc nostrils and eyes;

The hippopotamus (I) is made from grey cardboard, with black cardboard for the nostrils and eyes and white micro for the teeth;

The giraffe (J) is made from brown cardboard, with black cardboard for the spots and the mouth, half pieces of black confetti for the eyes and nostrils, black pieces of confetti for the ears and a strip of fringed black cardboard for the mane;

The cow (K) is made from brown cardboard, with black cardboard for the spot under the eye, white pieces of confetti for the eyes and felt pen for the pupils. The snout is made from kraft micro with black pieces of confetti for the nostrils;

The rhinoceros (L) is made from grey cardboard, with white confetti for the eye and black felt for the pupil, white micro for the tusk and mouth and half pieces of black confetti for the nostril;

The panda (M) is made from white micro with black cardboard for the ears, nose and outer part of the eye and white pieces of confetti and black felt pen for the eyes;

The cat (N) is made from black cardboard, with kraft micro for the muzzle and two punched holes for the inner part of the eyes;

The lion (0) is made from brown cardboard, with black cardboard for the mouth and nose and black pieces of confetti for the eyes.

Noah's ark – actual size templates

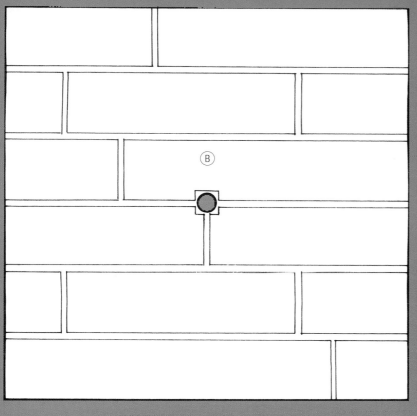

Noah's ark – actual size templates, except A, B and
C, which need to be enlarged x 205%

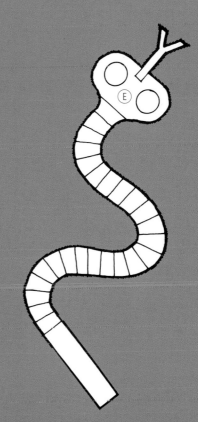

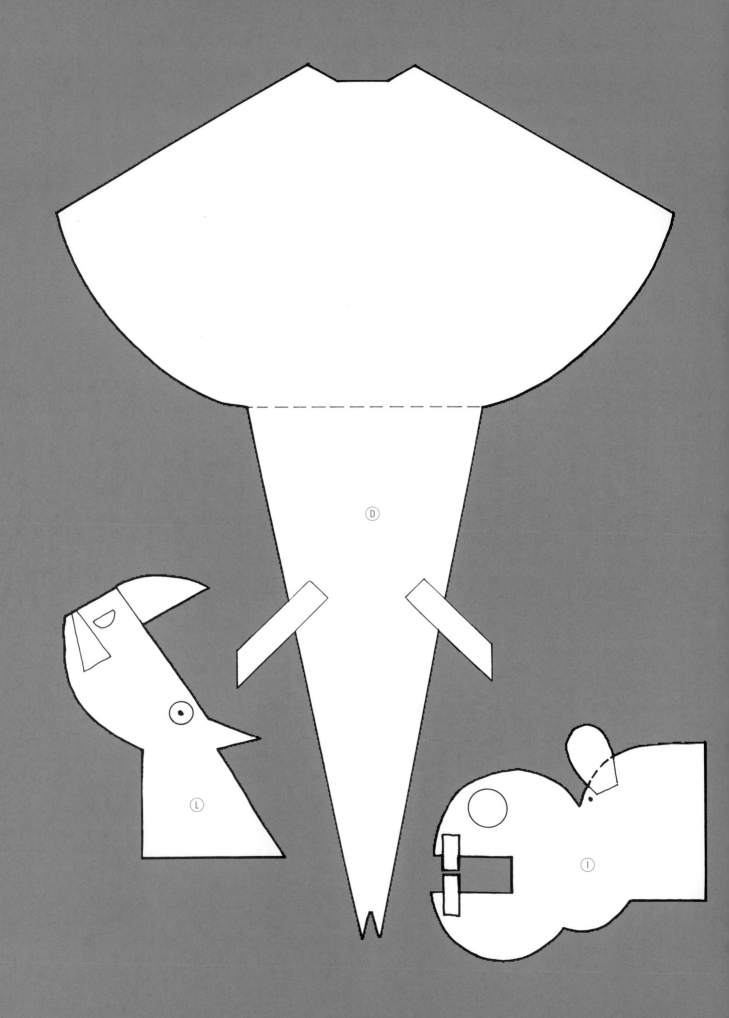

Pig

1
- **Draw and cut out** two body profiles (A) from 0.6 cardboard, cutting one out along the dotted lines. Attach the hooks onto the back of the complete profile. Glue the profiles to each other.
- **Draw and cut out** a body profile (B) from flexible cardboard and glue it onto the body.
- **Cut out** two 28 x 1.5cm (11 x ⁵⁄₈in) strips from 0.6 cardboard. Glue together, then glue them onto the bottom of the profile, between the legs.

SUPPLIES
· 0.6 cardboard: 100 x 100cm (40 x 40in)
· Flexible cardboard: 50 x 50cm (20 x 20in)
· Kraft micro: 30 x 30cm (12 x 12in)
· Black micro: 30 x 5cm (12 x 2in)
· Two frame hooks

2
- **Draw and cut out** one front leg (C) and one back leg (D) from 0.6 cardboard.
- **Cover** the legs in flexible cardboard (with the direction of the grooves facing in the opposite way to those on the body). Glue the legs onto the body.

Pig

And her four little ones with their useful hangers.

3
- **Snout**: Cut out one 5 x 11cm (2 x 4½in) rectangle from 0.6 cardboard and one 11 x 8.5cm (4¼ x 3¼in) rectangle from flexible cardboard. Bend and glue the flexible cardboard rectangle onto the other one. Cut one end at an angle (Diagram 1).
- **Draw and cut out** an oval (E) from kraft micro. Glue it onto the angled part of the snout and decorate with small spirals of black micro for the nostrils.
- **Glue** the snout onto the body (Diagram 2).

4
- **Ears:** Draw and cut out the ears (F and G) from kraft micro. Glue one ear behind the head, fold the other over the thickness of the body (following the dotted lines) and glue onto the front of the body.

5
- **Eyes:** Cut out two 13 x 0.5cm (5 x ¼in) strips of black micro, roll them up into spirals and glue them between the ears.

6
- **Tail:** Curl a 1 x 5cm (³⁄₈ x 2in) strip of flexible cardboard and glue it to the end of the body.

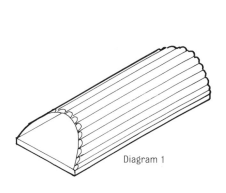

Diagram 1

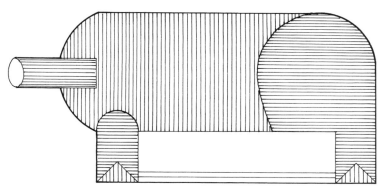

Diagram 2

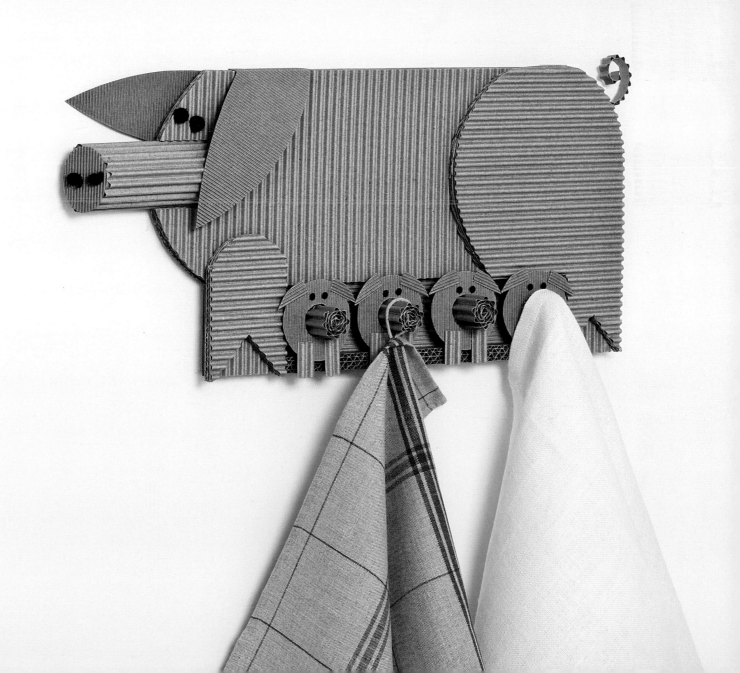

Pig (continued)

Little pig hangers

7 · **Make** four cylinders using four 22 x 5cm (8¾ x 2in) strips of flexible cardboard. Cut out four 50 x 2.5cm (20 x 1in) rectangles from flexible cardboard. Roll the rectangles up and glue them around the cylinders (Diagram 3).

8
· **Body:** Cut out four 6.5cm (2½in) circles from kraft micro and cut out a 2.5cm (1in) circle from their centres.
· **Decorate** each body with two ears made from kraft micro, two rectangles for the legs made from flexible cardboard and two pieces of confetti for the eyes made from black micro (H).

9 · **Insert and glue** the little pigs' bodies onto the pegs.
· **Glue** the pegs in the space under the pig's body, ensuring that they are evenly spaced.

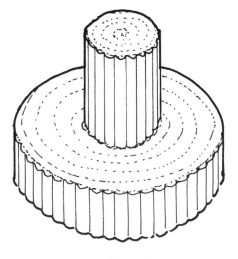

Diagram 3

Pig – Templates to be enlarged x 400% except E and H, which are actual size

Decorative objects

SUPPLIES

· 0.6 cardboard: 40 x 40cm (16 x 16in)

· 0.3 cardboard: 30 x 30cm (12 x 12in)

· Kraft micro: 40 x 10cm (16 x 4in)

· Black micro: 5 x 5cm (2 x 2in)

· Brown spray paint can

· Protective adhesive tape

Body and legs

1

· **Draw and cut out** 12 body profiles (A) from 0.6 cardboard. Glue them together in two sets of four.

Wise monkeys

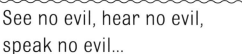

See no evil, hear no evil, speak no evil...

2

· **Draw and cut out** 12 profiles of the back leg (B) in 0.3 cardboard. Glue them together in six pairs, then glue them to either side of each body.

· **Cover** the curved edges of the legs with strips of kraft micro. Glue protective adhesive tape 2cm (¾in) above the bodies, where the noses will be placed (Diagram 1).

3

· **Draw and cut out** the profile of the front leg (C) from 0.3 cardboard. Fold the profiles, following the dotted lines from one side to other (Diagram 2).

· **Glue** the front legs onto the bodies in two positions: twice with the shoulders facing the top (D) and once with the shoulders facing the bottom (E).

· **Spray-paint** the three body profiles brown, ensuring that the paint penetrates into the grooves.

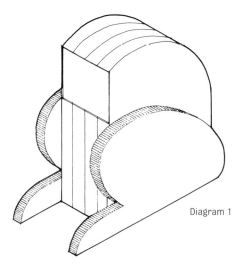

Diagram 1

Diagram 2

Decorative objects > **44**

Wise monkeys (continued)

Faces, feet and hands

4
- **Make three cones** from 40 x 0.7cm (16 x ¼in) strips of kraft micro for the mouths and noses.
- **Glue** a piece of confetti decorated with two black sticks to the top of each cone for the nostrils.
- **Glue** a small black curved strip below the nose for the mouth.
- **Remove** the adhesive tapes at the top of the bodies, then glue the cones onto these tapes.

5
- **Cut out** six 1.5cm (⁵⁄₈in) circles for the ears from kraft micro. Make a slit on either side of each head and insert the ears in place.

6
- **Cut out** six 1.2cm (½in) circles for the eyes from kraft micro, add pieces of black confetti for the pupils, then glue them into place above the nose (Diagram 3).

7
- **Feet and hands:** Cut out 12 rectangles measuring 2 x 0.8cm (¾ x ³⁄₈in) from kraft micro. Make several 1cm (³⁄₈in) cuts in the rectangles to form the fingers. Glue them onto the front and back legs. After drying, position the hands by gluing them onto the eyes, ears (D) and mouth (E).

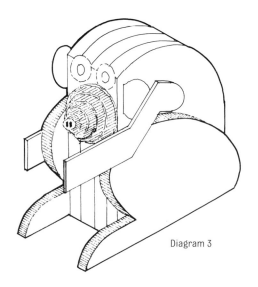

Diagram 3

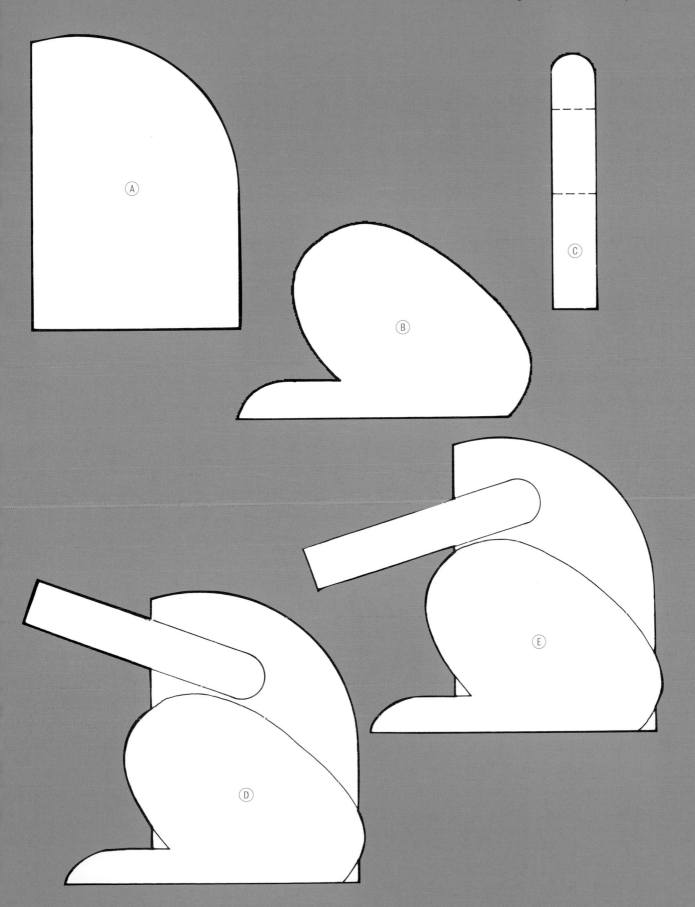

SUPPLIES

· 0.6 cardboard: 25 x 25cm (10 x 10in)

· Kraft micro: 5 x 5cm (2 x 2in)

· Black micro: 10 x 10cm (4 x 4in)

· Flexible cardboard: one-groove section

· Two black mini-beads

Body and legs

1
· **Draw and cut out** three body profiles from 0.6 cardboard (dotted lines), including one with the neck and head (A).
· **Glue** the profile with the neck and head between the two others (Diagram 1).
· **Draw, cut out and glue** the spots from black micro onto the body and neck (B).

2
· **Cut out** eight 12 x 0.7cm (4¾ x ¼in) strips for the legs from 0.6 cardboard. Glue them together in pairs, then cut them at an angle (C).
· **Cut out** a 6 x 1cm (2¼ x ³⁄₈in) strip from 0.6 cardboard. Cut it into four pieces for the hooves (D). Glue the hooves under the legs, and the legs onto either side of the body (Diagram 2).

Giraffe

The Greeks thought it was a combination of a camel and a leopard...

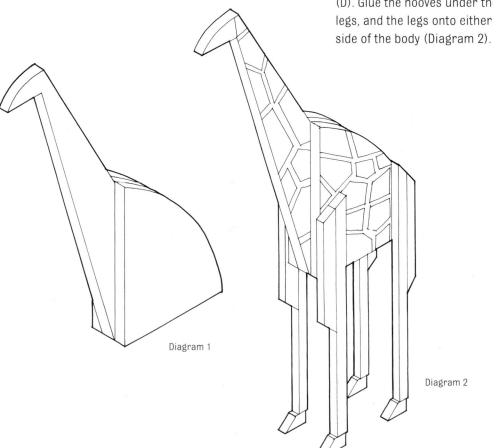

Diagram 1

Diagram 2

Giraffe (continued)

Head and tail

3 · **Make the head** as follows (Diagram 3):
(a): Cover the curve of the head with a strip of kraft micro cardboard;
(b): Glue the one-groove section of flexible cardboard under the head for the mouth;
(c): Glue on a piece of black confetti cut in half for the nostrils;
(d): Glue the two mini-beads in place for the eyes;
(e): Insert the two kraft micro ears (E), cut out in advance and folded along the dotted lines;
(f): Cut out and glue two sticks from kraft micro for the horns, each with half a piece of black confetti glued on top.

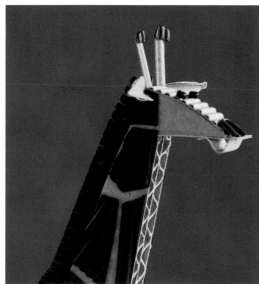

4 · **Cut out** a 9 x 1.5cm (3½ x ⅝in) strip of black micro for the mane (F). Fold it into two along the dotted lines and cut a 5mm (¼in) deep fringe on either side. Glue the mane onto the neck.

5 · **Cut out** a 5 x 0.7cm (2 x ¼in) strip from 0.6 cardboard for the tail. Wrap it in a 3cm (1¼in) square of black micro with a fringe on one side and cut it at an angle on the opposite side. Glue it onto the angle at the back of the body.

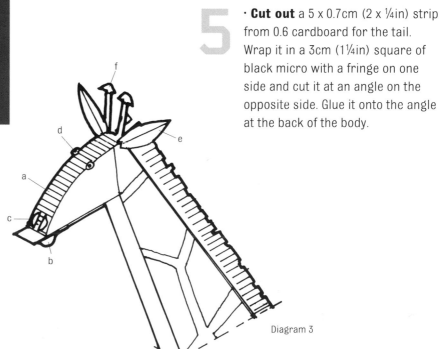

Diagram 3

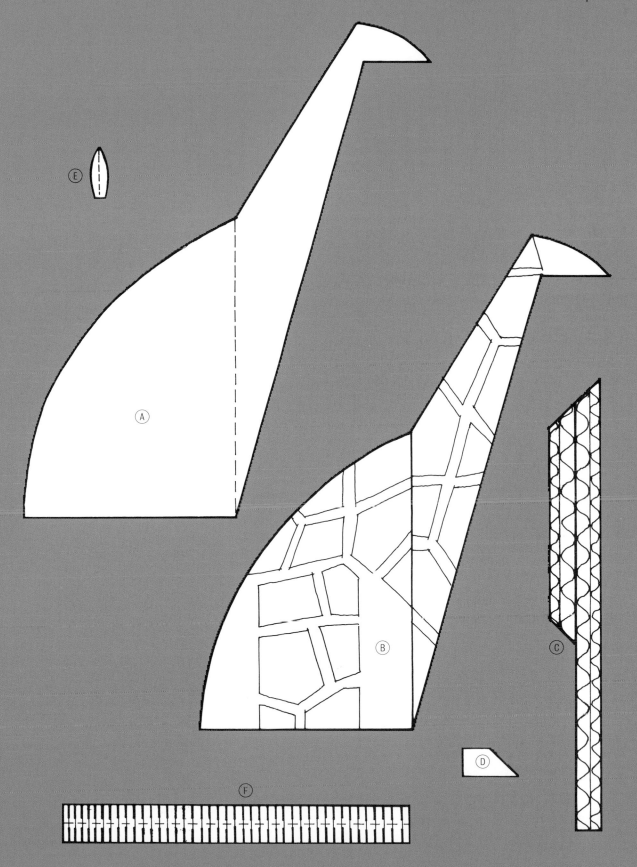

SUPPLIES

· 0.6 cardboard: 20 x 20cm (8 x 8in)

· Kraft micro: 20 x 10cm (8 x 4in)

· Blue micro: 20 x 10cm (8 x 4in)

· Thick paper: 20 x 20cm (8 x 8in)

· Grey/green spray paint

· Nylon thread

Body and head

1

· **Cut out** a 19 x 0.7cm (7½ x ¼in) stick and two 13.5 x 0.7cm (5³⁄₈ x ¼in) sticks from 0.6 cardboard. Glue together as indicated in (A).

· **Make a cut** into the thickness of the top and bottom bands as indicated by the dots, then cut the two sides at an angle along the dotted line.

Dragonfly

A design by nature, unchanged in 300 million years...

2

· **Glue together** the various elements that make up the body (B):

(a): On the top, regularly spaced, the small rectangles of blue micro;

(b): On either side, two 5.5 x 0.7cm (2¼ x ¼in) sticks, cut out from 0.6 cardboard and cut at an angle at each end;

(c): At the front, a spiral made from a 22 x 0.5cm (8¾ x ¼in) strip of kraft micro;

(d): At the tip, a piece of blue micro cut out in the shape of a Y.

3

· **Make a cone** for the head with a 25 x 0.5cm (10 x ¼in) strip of kraft micro:

(e): Insert and glue it to the end of the body;

(f): Make two mini-spirals from blue micro with two smaller mini-spirals from kraft micro on top for the eyes.

Dragonfly (continued)

Wings and legs

4
· **Cut out** 24 sticks measuring 16 x 0.3cm (6½ x ⅛in) from 0.6 cardboard. Glue them together to form the ribs in the wings.
· **Draw and cut out** two pairs of wings (C) from thick paper. Position the ribbed section on the drawing and cut out, following the wing shape. Spray-paint the wings grey/green.
· **Make** two small cylinders using two 2cm (¾in) squares of kraft micro. Glue the wings onto the edges of the body using the small cylinders to incline them (Diagram 1).

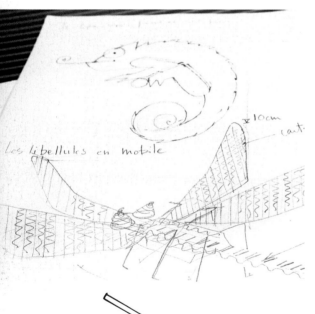

5
· **Cut out** three thin strips of blue micro, 12cm (4¾in) in length, to make the legs.
· **Slip** the legs into position and glue them into the grooves under the wings.
· **Fold** the legs twice on either side, alternating the direction of folding.

6
· **Hang** the dragonfly with nylon thread.

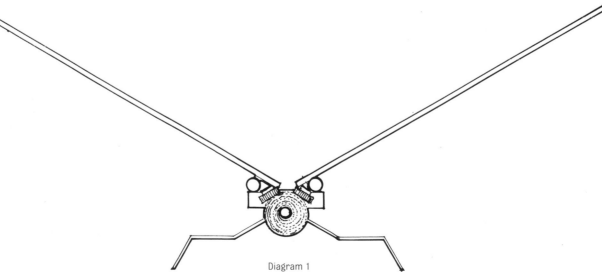

Diagram 1

Dragonfly – actual size templates

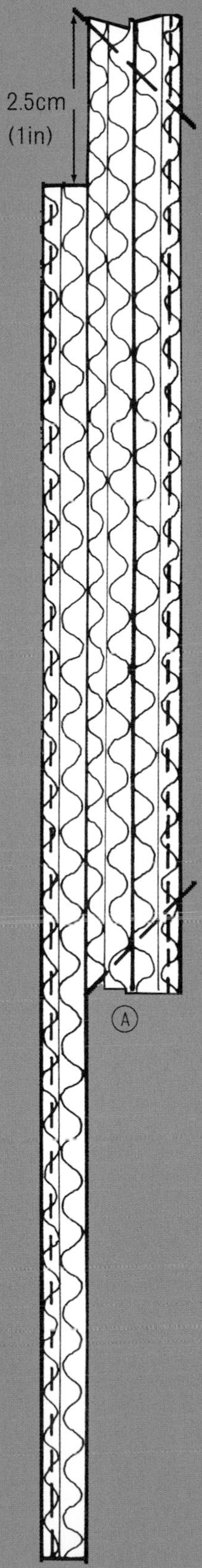

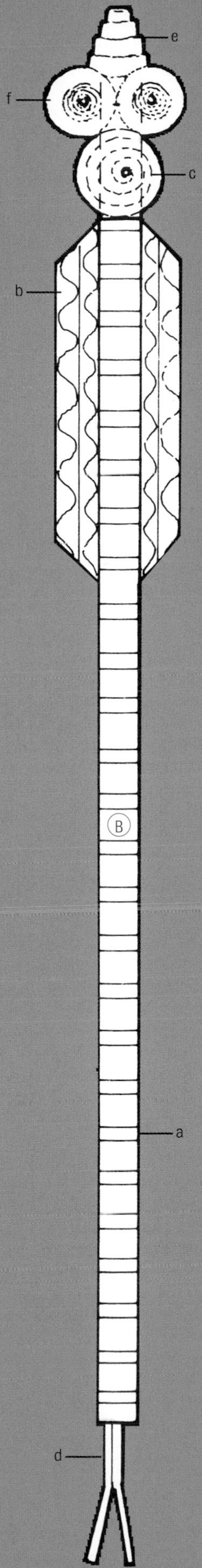

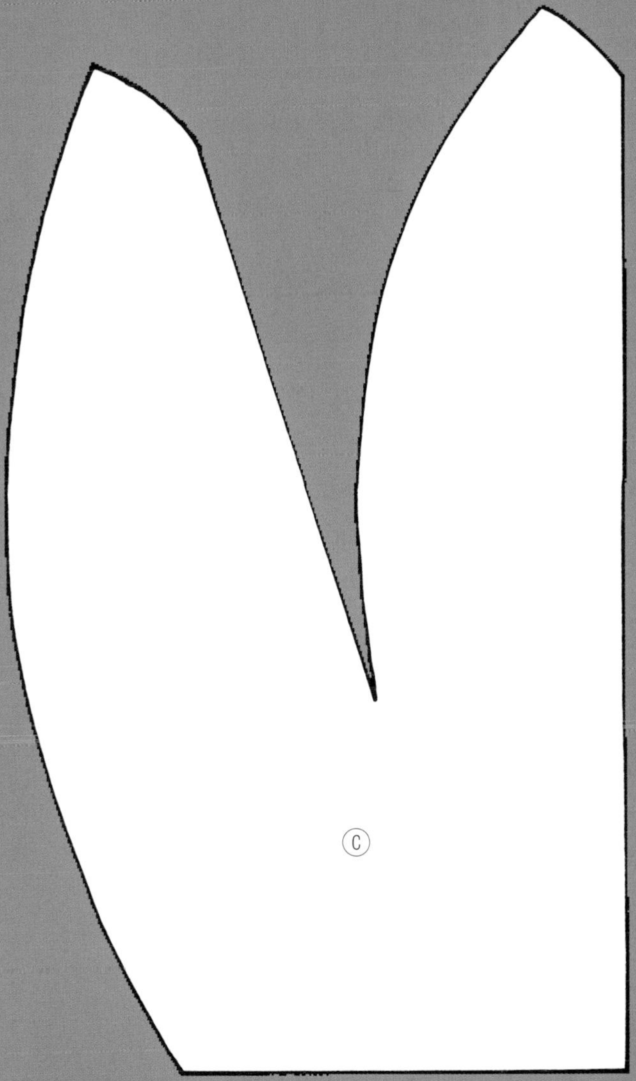

2.5cm
(1in)

e

f

c

b

Ⓐ

Ⓑ

a

d

Ⓒ

SUPPLIES

· 0.6 cardboard: 20 x 20cm (8 x 8in)

· Flexible cardboard: 30 x 30cm
(12 x 12in)

· Kraft micro: 30 x 30cm (12 x 12in)

Body and tail

1
· **Draw and cut out** two body profiles from 0.6 cardboard (A) and glue them together.
· **Cover** each side of the body with kraft micro.

2
· **Draw and cut out** two tail profiles (B) from kraft micro.
· **Glue** them onto each side of the body, starting from the dotted lines (A).
· **Glue** the two round parts of the tail together.

Chameleon

Brown on the sand, grey on the rocks, green in the grass...

3
· **Make** the various elements that decorate the body (Diagram 1):
(a): Cut out and glue a 1.4cm (⅝in) wide strip of flexible cardboard underneath the body;
(b) and (c): Cut out a 2.5cm (1in) wide strip of flexible cardboard, flatten the grooves with a ruler and glue a piece onto the head, letting the strip extend past each side of the body. Glue the other piece onto the back and tail;
(d): Attach a 6mm (¼in) wide flattened strip to the thickness, extending from either side of the back and tail;
(e): Roll up and glue the end of the strip into a spiral shape.

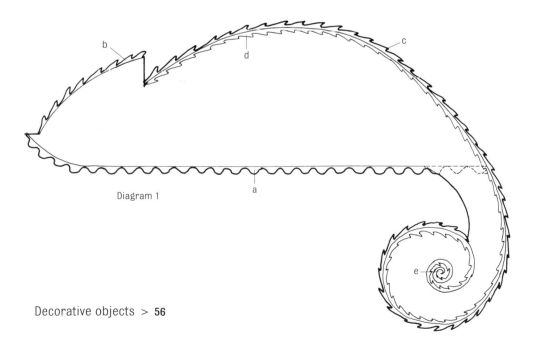

Diagram 1

Chameleon (continued)

Legs and head

4
· **Cut out** eight 10 x 0.7cm (4 x ¼in) sticks from 0.6 cardboard for the legs.
· **Glue** the sticks together in pairs to form four legs.
· **Cut one** end of each leg at a 45° angle and four others in a Y shape (C). Cut the front legs a little shorter.
· **Fold and glue** the legs in a staggered position on each side of the body.

5
· **Make** two cones from kraft micro. Glue them onto the head for the eyes.
· **Cut out** a small strip from kraft micro for the mouth. Fold in an accordion shape and glue in place.
· **Cut out** a thin, 20cm (8in) long strip from kraft micro for the tongue. Roll it up into a spiral and glue it in position onto the mouth.

6
· **Cut out** 7mm (¼in) wide strips from flexible cardboard. Remove each strip and glue them flat and in profile onto the sides of the body for the scales.

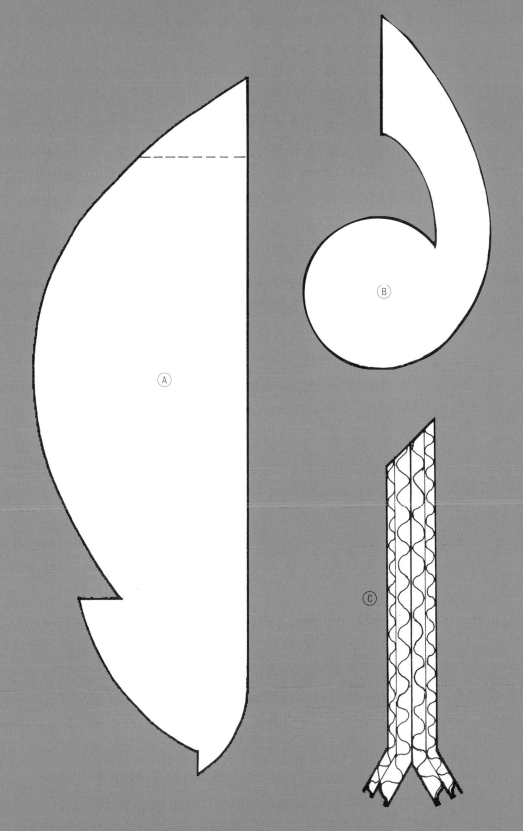

SUPPLIES

· 0.3 cardboard: 50 x 50cm (20 x 20in)

· 0.6 cardboard: 30 x 30cm (12 x 12in)

· Flexible cardboard: 50 x 50cm (20 x 20in)

· Kraft micro: 5 x 5cm (2 x 2in)

· Black micro: 5 x 5cm (2 x 2in)

Body and head

1

· **Draw and cut out** two body profiles (A) from 0.3 cardboard.

· **Cut out** six 10cm (4in) squares from 0.6 cardboard, including two cut-outs at a right angle, the size of a quarter of the square.

Camel

The Bedouins call them 'ships of the desert'...

2

· **Draw and cut out** two head profiles (B) from 0.3 cardboard.

· **Cut out and glue** a square (C) from 0.6 cardboard onto one of the profiles. Glue the other head profile onto the square.

3

· **Glue** two full squares onto a body profile. Glue two cut-out squares (Step 1) onto the two full squares (Diagram 1).

· **Glue** the head onto the cut-out corner (Diagram 2), then glue on the two remaining full squares.

· **Glue** the second body profile onto the unit.

4

· **Cut out and glue** a 4.5cm (1¾in) wide strip of flexible cardboard all around the body.

· **Seal** the sides of the neck with two more narrow strips.

· **Cut out and glue** a 1.5cm (⅝in) wide strip of flexible cardboard all around the head and neck (Diagram 3). Ensure that the grooves are flattened on top of the head, using a ruler.

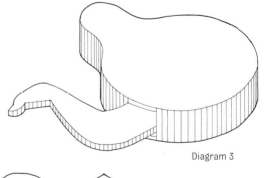

Diagram 3

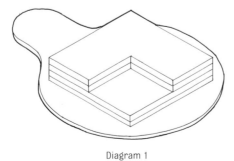

Diagram 1

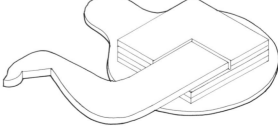

Diagram 2

Camel (continued)

6

Legs, face and tail

5

· **Draw and cut out** four front leg (D) and four rear leg profiles (E) from 0.3 cardboard.
· **Cut out** eight 21 x 1cm (8¼ x ³⁄₈in) sticks from 0.6 cardboard (F). Glue them together in pairs. Glue each double stick between two leg profiles (Diagram 4).
· **Cut out and glue** a 1.6cm (½in) strip of flexible cardboard around each leg.

· **Draw and cut out** eight hoof profiles (G) from 0.6 cardboard. Cut out four triangles following the dotted lines.
· **Glue** the end of each leg between two hoof profiles, adding a triangle in the middle (Diagram 5). Glue the legs onto the body, ensuring that they are balanced.

7

· **Draw and cut out** two ears (D) from kraft micro. Slip them into place and glue them onto the notches made in the head.
· **Make** three pieces of confetti from black micro, glue two folded pieces into place for the eyes and cut one in two for the nostrils.
· **Glue** on a small strip of black micro for the mouth.

8

· **Cut out** a 10 x 0.7cm (4 x ¼in) stick for the tail from 0.6 cardboard. Create a 3cm (1¼in) fringe and glue it to the back of the body.

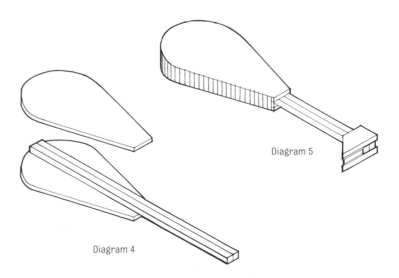

Diagram 5

Diagram 4

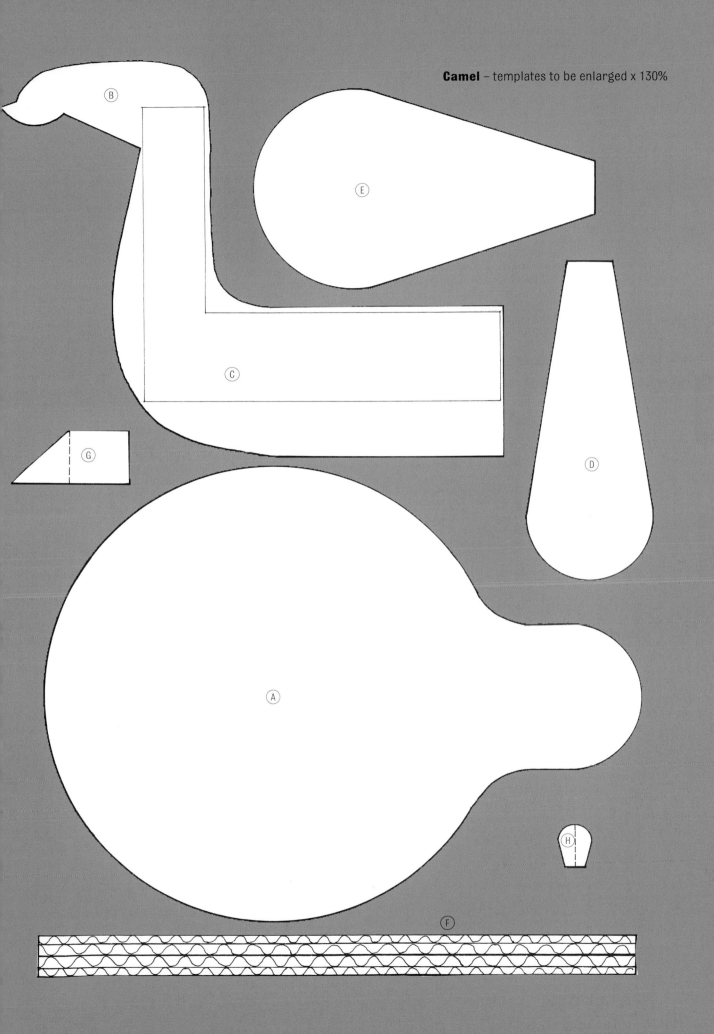

Camel – templates to be enlarged x 130%

Body and head

SUPPLIES
· Semi-cylindrical lampshade frame
· 25W low-energy bulb
· Sheet of transparent polyphane
· 0.6 cardboard: 30 x 30cm (12 x 12in)
· Flexible cardboard: 50 x 50cm
(20 x 20in)
· Kraft micro: 8 x 8cm (3¼ x 3¼in)
· Two 1.5cm (⅝in) brown wooden beads

1
· **The body:** Cut out 32 sticks measuring
0.7 x 22cm (8¾ x ¼in) from 0.6 cardboard.
· **Glue** together in pairs (large groove against
large groove), then glue around the rounded
edges of the lamp shade frame, ensuring that the
sticks are perpendicular to the support. Apply a
polyphane sheet to the interior curve of the body.

2
· **Wings:** Draw and cut out two
profiles (A) from flexible cardboard.
Glue them to each side of the body.

Owl

Native Americans believe they provide
help and protection at night...

3
· **Legs:** Cut out six leg profiles
(B) from 0.6 cardboard.
Glue them in sets of three
(Diagram 1), then glue to the
bottom of the body.

4

· **Eyes:** Make two spirals with 26 x 0.7cm (10½ x ¼in) strips of flexible cardboard.
Glue the beads to the centre of the spirals. Glue the eyes to the top of the body.
· **Beak:** Draw and cut out the beak profile (C) from 0.6 cardboard. Cover it with kraft
micro, fold it slightly and glue it between the two eyes.
· **Crests:** Cut out two 8 x 0.8cm (3¼ x ³⁄₈in) rectangles from kraft micro. Divide them
in two up to 4cm (1¾in), then slot them into place and glue above the eyes.

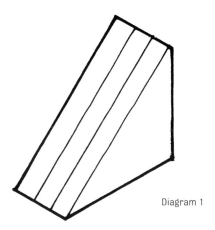

Diagram 1

Owl – templates to be enlarged x 200%

SUPPLIES

· 0.6 cardboard: 80 x 80cm (32 x 32in)

· Flexible cardboard: 1 x 1m (40 x 40in)

· Kraft micro: 50 x 50cm (20 x 20in)

· Black micro: 50 x 50cm (20 x 20in)

· Gilded paper: 10 x 10cm (4 x 4in)

· 56 black mini-beads

· Rubber strips

Chessboard and parts

1 · **The box**: Cut out a 30cm (12in) square bottom and 30.7 x 10cm (12¼ x 4in) rectangular sides from 0.6 cardboard. Glue the sides to the bottom (Diagram 1).

The zoo

A uniquely decorative chessboard with animals for all the pieces.

2 · **Chessboard:** Cut out two squares: 40cm (16in) and 30cm (12in) from 0.6 cardboard. Glue the smaller square onto the centre of the larger one.
· **Trace** the chessboard onto the larger square, each chess square 5 x 5cm (2 x 2in).
· **Cut out** 32 squares of 5 x 5cm (2 x 2in) from 0.6 cardboard. Glue them in staggered rows, smooth sides outward.
· **Cut out** 32 sticks measuring 35 x 0.7cm (14 x ¼in) from 0.6 cardboard. Cut each stick into seven 5cm (2in) pieces. Glue seven sticks in each empty box (Diagram 2).

3 · **Parts:** Make 32 cylinders from 32 rectangles, 21cm (8¼in) in length. The width differs depending on the piece:
- two kings, two queens (lions and lionesses): four cylinders (21 x 6.5cm [8¼ x 2⅝in]);
- four knights (horses), four rooks (owls): eight cylinders (21 x 6cm [8¼ x 2½in]);
- four bishops (monkeys): four cylinders (21 x 5cm [8¼ x 2in]);
- 16 pawns (mice): 16 cylinders (21 x 4cm [8¼ x 1¾in]).
· **Wrap** 16 pieces in kraft micro and the other 16 in black micro.
· **Hold** in place with elastic bands while drying.

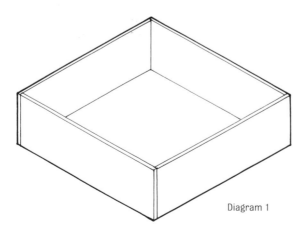

Diagram 1

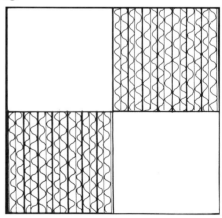

Diagram 2

The zoo (continued)

The pieces (continued)

4 · **Lions and lionesses:** Cut out four 10 x 1.5cm (4 x ⅝in) strips of flexible cardboard. Glue them to the base of the four cylinders. Wrap two in strips of kraft micro and two in strips of black micro. Draw, cut out and glue the decorative elements from kraft micro or black micro, based on the pairs (A, B, C, D, E, F, G for the lion; A, B, C, D, E for the lioness). Cut slots in the cylinders for the ears.

5 · **Monkeys:** Make four cones with four 23 x 0.7cm (9¼ x ¼in) strips of flexible cardboard; the grooves of which have been flattened beforehand using a ruler. Glue the cones onto the cylinders at the position of the nose (H). Draw, cut out and glue the decorative elements from kraft micro (I, J, K). Cut slots in the cylinders for the ears.

6 · **Horses:** Draw, cut out and glue the decorative elements made from kraft micro and black micro (L, M, N) onto the cylinders. Fold the mane along the dotted line then create a fringe. The snout is made from flexible cardboard.

7 · **Owls:** Make four spirals with four 20 x 0.5cm (8 x ¼in) strips of kraft micro (O). Glue them onto the cylinders. Draw, cut out and glue the decorative elements made from kraft micro and black micro (P, Q). Cut slots in the cylinders for the ears.

8 · **Mice:** Make 16 cones with eight 20 x 0.5cm (8 x ¼in) strips of kraft micro and eight strips of black micro. Glue them onto the cylinders (R). Draw, cut out and glue the decorative elements made from kraft micro and black micro (S, T, U). Create a fringe for the whiskers and fold.

SUPPLIES
· **0.6 cardboard: 70 x 70cm (28 x 28in)**
· **Flexible cardboard: 30 x 30cm (12 x 12in)**
· **Foamboard: 40 x 20cm (16 x 8in)**
· **Kraft micro: 30 x 30cm (12 x 12in)**
· **White micro: 30 x 20cm (12 x 8in)**
· **Blue micro: 20 x 20cm (8 x 8in)**
· **Four pins**
· **Hook for frame**

Box

1

· **Cut out** the 32cm (12¾in) square bottom from 0.6 cardboard. Cut out three rectangular sides:
(a) 31.3 x 4cm (12³⁄₈ x 1¾in) twice and (b) 32 x 4cm (12¾ x 1¾in) once.
· **Glue** the rectangles against the bottom (Diagram 1). Attach the hook in the middle of the bottom.
· **Cut out** a 32cm (12¾in) square from flexible cardboard. Glue it onto the bottom.

Butterflies

A curiosity cabinet collection box guaranteed to have a decorative effect!

2

· **Cut out** two 36cm (14¼in) squares: one from foamboard and the other from 0.6 cardboard. Hollow out a 26cm (10¼in) square in the centre of each to create the frame. Glue them one on top of the other. Decorate the white side of the foamboard by gluing four 26 x 0.3cm (10¼ x ⅛in) sticks made from 0.6 cardboard all the way around the window.
· **Glue** a small spiral of kraft micro to each corner and decorate the width of the window with four 26 x 1cm (10¼ x ³⁄₈in) strips of white micro.
· **Glue** the frame onto the bottom; the open part of this being directed upwards to let the light in.

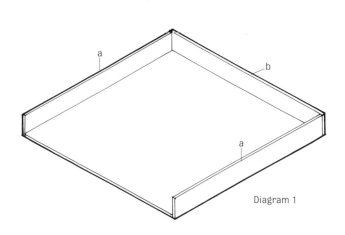

Diagram 1

Butterflies (continued)

4

Brown butterfly

3 · **Wings:** Fold a 10 x 15cm (4 x 6in) rectangle of kraft micro with the corrugated sides facing each other. Draw a wing on a folded side (A) and cut out both sides simultaneously with scissors. Unfold the wings.

· **Make** the elements for the body (Diagram 2):
(a): Cut out a 6 x 3cm (2¼ x 1¼in) rectangle from kraft micro. Roll it up and glue it. Glue it to the centre of the wings.
(b): Cut out and fold a 13 x 0.3cm (5¼ x ⅛in) strip of kraft micro. Glue it under the cylinder and decorate it with a 4 x 0.3cm (1¾ x ⅛in) strip of kraft micro glued flat.
(c) and (d): Make and glue together a small spiral for the head and a 3cm (1¼in) strip of kraft micro divided into two for the antennae.

5 · **Reproduce** the drawings of the decorations (B) on the wings.
· **Cut out** fine 2mm (⅛in) wide strips of kraft micro and blue micro. Shape them by crushing, rolling up, curling and folding them, according to the motifs.
· **Apply glue** to them and place them carefully onto the decorative drawings using tweezers. Complete the drawings with pieces of blue confetti.

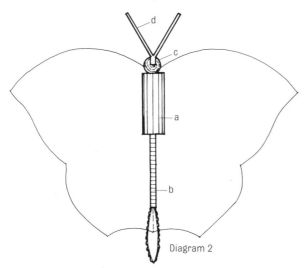

Diagram 2

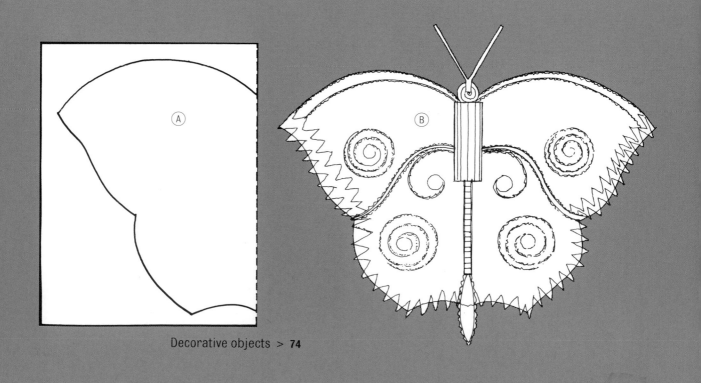

6 Blue butterfly

· **Wings:** Fold a 15 x 10cm (6 x 4in) rectangle of blue micro with the corrugated sides facing each other. Draw a wing on one folded side (C) and cut out both sides simultaneously with scissors. Unfold the wings.

7 · **Make** the elements for the body (Diagram 3):
(a): Cut out a 5.5 x 2cm (2¼ x ¾in) rectangle from kraft micro. Roll up into a cylinder and glue. Roll a 4 x 2cm (1¾ x ¾in) rectangle of kraft micro around the cylinder, 5mm (⅛in) from one end. Glue to the centre of the wings.
(b): Decorate the body with fine blue strips. Insert a small strip at the end of this.
(c): Glue two blue spots in place for the eyes and a folded fine strip for the antennae.

8 · **Reproduce** the drawings of the decorations (D) on the wings.
· **Cut out** fine 2mm (⅛in) wide strips of kraft micro. Shape the strips by crushing, rolling up, curling and folding them, according to the motifs.
· **Apply glue** to them and place them carefully onto the decorative drawings using tweezers. Complete the drawings with pieces of confetti.

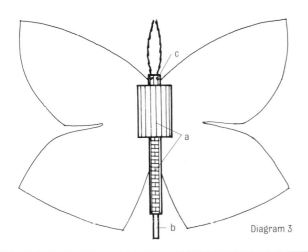

Diagram 3

Butterflies – templates to be enlarged x 130%

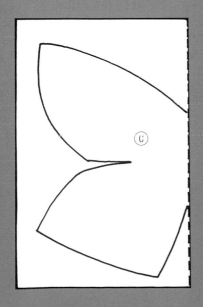

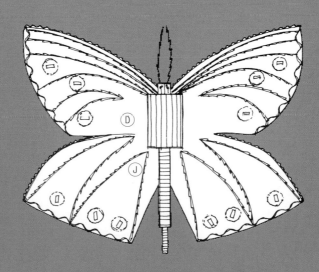

Butterflies (continued)

White butterfly

9 · **Draw the wings:** Fold an 11 x 12cm (4¼ x 4¾in) rectangle of white micro with corrugated sides facing each other. Draw a wing on one folded side (E) and cut out both sides simultaneously with scissors. Unfold.

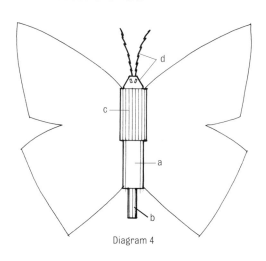

Diagram 4

10 · **Make** the elements for the body (Diagram 4):
(a): Cut out a 6cm (2¼in) strip of flexible cardboard. Cut out two strips at an angle at one end for the head. Glue the strip to the centre of the wings.
(b): Insert a piece of kraft micro into the hollow part under the strip.
(c): Cut out and glue a 2.5 x 1.5cm (1 x ⅝in) rectangle of kraft micro onto the strip.
(d): Glue two blue dots for the eyes and a small folded strip for the antennae in place.

11 · **Reproduce** the drawings of the decorations (F) on the wings.
· **Cut out** and flatten fine strips of flexible cardboard. Shape the strips by crushing, rolling up, curling and folding them, according to the motifs.
· **Apply glue** to them and place them carefully onto the decorative drawings using tweezers. Complete the drawings with pieces of confetti.

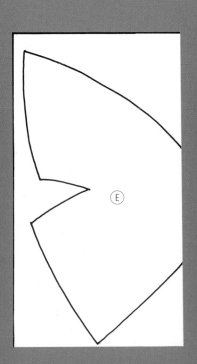

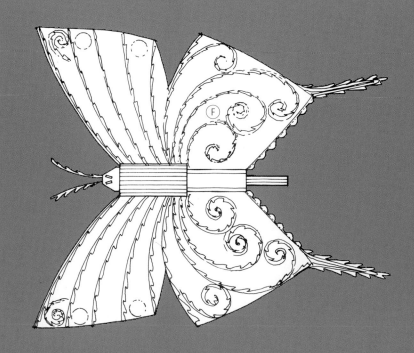

Large brown and blue butterfly

12

· **Wings:** Fold a 14.5 x 12cm (5¾ x 4¾in) rectangle of kraft micro with the corrugated sides facing each other. Draw a wing on one folded side (G) and cut out both sides simultaneously with scissors. Unfold.

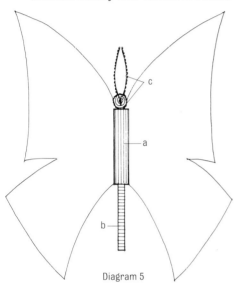

Diagram 5

13

· **Make** the elements for the body (Diagram 5):
(a): Cut out a 6 x 4cm (2¼ x 1¾in) rectangle of blue micro. Roll up it and glue to it to the centre of the wings.
(b): Glue a fine strip of blue micro, folded in two, to one end.
(c): Make a small spiral of blue micro for the head and a small folded strip of blue micro for the antennae and glue into place.

14

· **Reproduce** the drawings of the decorations (H) on the wings.
· **Cut out** and flatten fine strips of blue micro. Shape the strips by crushing, rolling up, curling and folding them, according to the motifs.
· **Apply** glue to them and place them carefully onto the decorative drawings using tweezers. Complete the drawings with pieces of confetti.

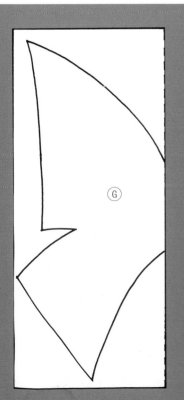

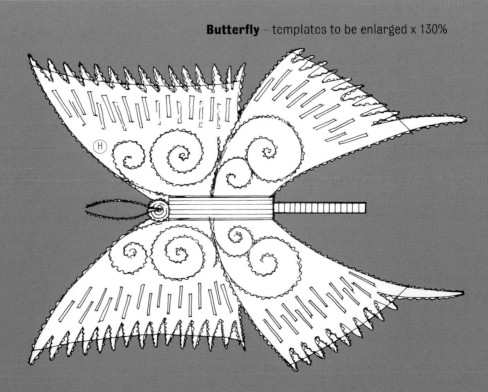

Butterfly – templates to be enlarged x 130%

Bracket and head

1

· **Trace** the quarter of an oval (A) and use it to reproduce a whole oval on 0.6 cardboard.
· **Cut out** the oval and fix two frame hooks onto it for hanging.
· **Cover** with black micro.
· **Cut out and glue** around a flexible strip of cardboard, 1cm ($^3/_8$in) in width.

Moose head

A hunting trophy that doesn't take itself at all seriously!

SUPPLIES

· 0.6 cardboard: 1 x 1m (40 x 40in)
· 0.3 cardboard: 30 x 30cm (12 x 12in)
· 0.1 cardboard: 70 x 30cm (28 x 12in)
· Flexible cardboard: 40 x 40cm (16 x 16in)
· Kraft micro: 20 x 10cm (8 x 4in)
· Black micro: 30 x 30cm (12 x 12in)
· Two 1.5cm ($^5/_8$in) brown wooden beads
· Two frame hooks
· Two pins

2

· **Draw and cut out** two head profiles (B) from 0.6 cardboard. Cut out two 20 x 13cm (8 x 5¼in) rectangles (a) from 0.6 cardboard and one 30 x 14.4cm (12 x 5¾in) rectangle (b) from 0.3 cardboard. Glue the two (a) rectangles together.
· **Glue** two profiles (B) to (a) (Diagram 1).
· **Cut out** three 14cm (5½in) squares from 0.6 cardboard. Glue them together, then glue in place behind the head.
· **Cut out** two 14.4 x 2.5cm (5¾ x 1in) rectangles (c) from 0.6 cardboard. Glue them together, then glue them in place onto the top of the head.
· **Glue** rectangle (b) onto the sides at an angle to the head (Diagram 2).

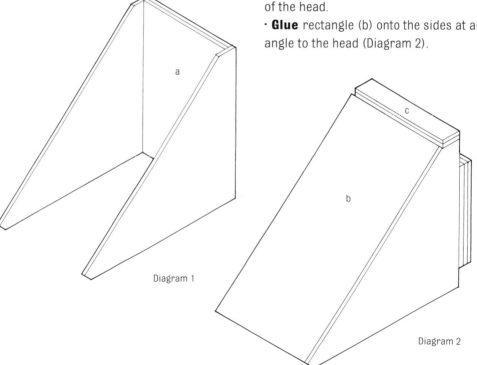

Diagram 1

Diagram 2

Moose head (continued)

Face and antlers

3 · **Draw** and cut out a snout (C) from 0.6 cardboard. Cover with flexible cardboard.
· **Draw, cut out and glue** two nostrils (D) made from black micro in place. Glue the snout at the bottom from the head and decorate it with a strip of flexible cardboard.

4 · **Cut out** a 17 x 10cm (6¾ x 4in) rectangle for the mane from flexible cardboard. Create a 14cm (5½in) fringe, fold into two, then glue to the interior under the head (Diagram 3).

5 · **Draw and cut out** two ears (E) from kraft micro. Lightly use a cutter to help fold along the dotted lines and glue the ears to each side of the head.

6 · **Make** two spirals for the eyes from two 19 x 0.7cm strips of flexible cardboard. Glue the beads to the centre of the spirals. Glue and pin the eyes onto the head (Diagram 4).

7 · **Draw and cut out** the nose (E) from 0.6 cardboard. Make a notch at the top of the head in front of the ears to slide the antlers in and glue them in place.

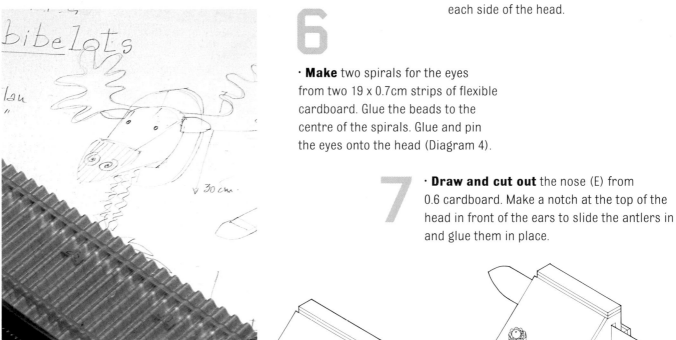

Diagram 3

Diagram 4

Moose head – actual size templates, except A, B, C, F, which are to be enlarged x 300%

SUPPLIES

· 0.6 cardboard: 1 x 1m (40 x 40in)
· Flexible cardboard: 50 x 50cm
(20 x 20in)
· Kraft micro: 30 x 30cm (12 x 12in)
· Black micro: 20 x 20cm (8 x 8in)
· White micro: 10 x 10cm (4 x 4in)
· Punch

Body and head

1
· **Draw and cut out** four body profiles (A) from 0.6 cardboard. Glue them together in two pairs.
· **Cut out** two 34 x 18cm (13½ x 7in) rectangles from 0.6 cardboard and glue them together.
· **Glue** the two blocks of body profiles on each side of the block of rectangles (Diagram 1).
· **Cut out** a 37 x 37.5cm (14¾ x 15in) rectangle from flexible cardboard. Glue it to the curve of the body (Diagram 2).

2
· **Draw and cut out** the head, which is a 22 x 12cm (8¾ x 4¾in) rectangle cut from 0.6 cardboard. Fold this in the middle of its length at a right angle.
· **Draw and cut out** two head profiles (B) and glue them to the folded rectangle (Diagram 3).
· **Cut out** a 17 x 12cm (6¾ x 4¾in) rectangle of kraft micro and glue it to the curve of the head.

3
· **Draw and cut out** two ears (C) from black micro. Glue them to the back of the head.
· **Draw and cut out** the two spots (D) of black micro. Glue them onto the head (Diagram 4).

Bulldog

He has a calm temperament and doesn't bark too much – making him the ideal companion!

4
· **Cut out** two 2.5cm (1in) circles from white micro for eyes.
· **Make** two spirals from two 15 x 0.5cm (5 x ¼in) strips of black micro.
· **Glue** the black spirals onto the white circles, then glue the eyes to the spots, raising them slightly.

5
· **Draw and cut out** the nose (E without the point) from 0.6 cardboard. Cover it with black micro (all of E).
· **Glue** the nose to the base of the spots.

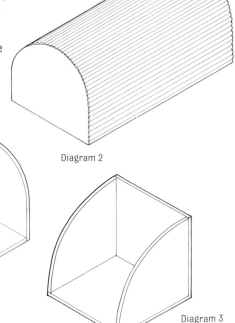

Diagram 2

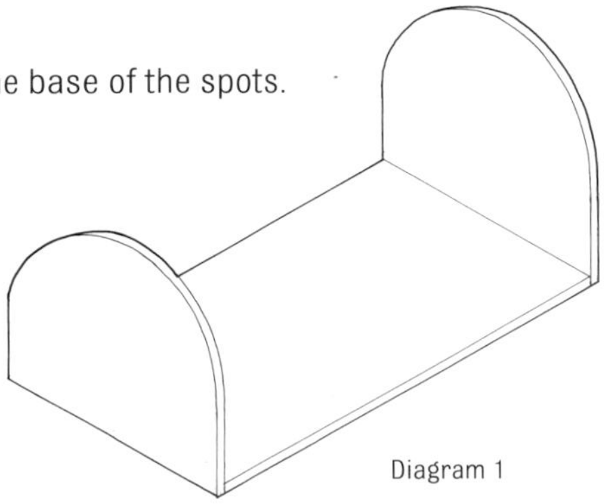

Diagram 1

Diagram 3

Bulldog (continued)

Mouth, legs and tail

6 · **Draw and cut out** the mouth (F) from kraft micro. Glue it in place, starting from the lower part of the head, bending it and sticking the end under the nose.
· **Cut out** two triangles (G) from white micro for teeth. Glue them at each side of the mouth.
· **Punch** holes on either side of the mouth, to represent the whiskers (Diagram 5).

7 · **Glue** the head onto the body.
· **Collar:** Glue a 3cm (1¼in) wide strip of black micro to the curve of the body behind the head. Draw and cut out nine triangles (H) from 0.6 cardboard to stick onto the collar.

8 · **Tail:** Draw and cut out two triangles (I) of black micro. Glue them to each other, then onto the back of the body (Diagram 6).

9 · **Draw and cut out** eight front leg profiles (J) and eight back leg profiles (K). Glue them together in two sets of four. Glue the leg blocks to the front and back of the body.

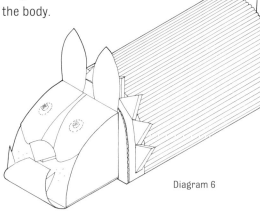

Diagram 6

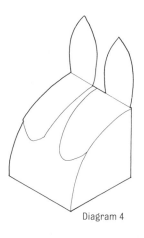

Diagram 4

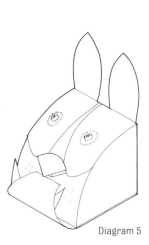

Diagram 5

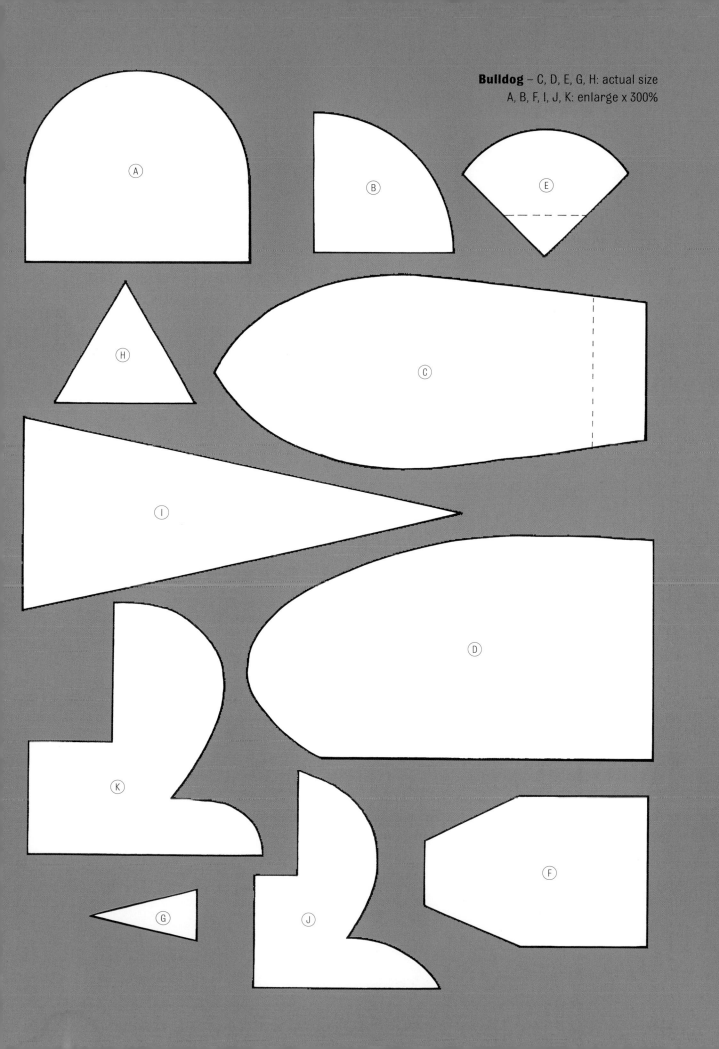

Bulldog – C, D, E, G, H: actual size
A, B, F, I, J, K: enlarge x 300%

Cardboard furniture

Body, head and legs

1

· **Draw and cut out** two body profiles (A) from 0.6 cardboard.

· **Cut out** rectangles from 0.6 cardboard: 12 x 27cm (4¾ x 10¾in) (a) and 12 x 7cm (4¾ x 2¾in) (c) once, and 12 x 30.7cm (4¾ x 12¾in) (b) twice. Glue together the two (b)s.

· **Glue** the rectangles onto a body profile in the correct position (Diagram 1).

· **Seal** the body together by gluing over the second body profile (Diagram 2).

Cow

Cute and comical, she's very useful for storing baby things!

2

· **Draw and cut out** the base of the head (B) from 0.6 cardboard.

· **Fold** the two sides of the head slightly inwards following the dotted lines (A). Glue the base between the two sides.

· **Draw and cut out** the rounded part of the head (C) from kraft micro. Glue the rounded part to the curves of the head.

3

· **Draw and cut out** six spots from black micro: (a), (b) (right profile), (c), (d) (face), (e) and (f) (left profile). Glue them onto the body.

4

· **Cut** the paper towel roll into four equal sections to form the legs. Glue them to each corner under the body and decorate one with black micro.

· **Cut out** four 33 x 8cm (13 x 3¼in) rectangles of flexible cardboard. Roll each one up into a spiral and slide them into each section of the roll, so that they stick out. Glue them into position.

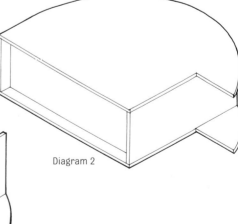

Diagram 2

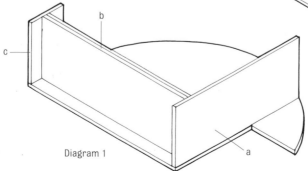

Diagram 1

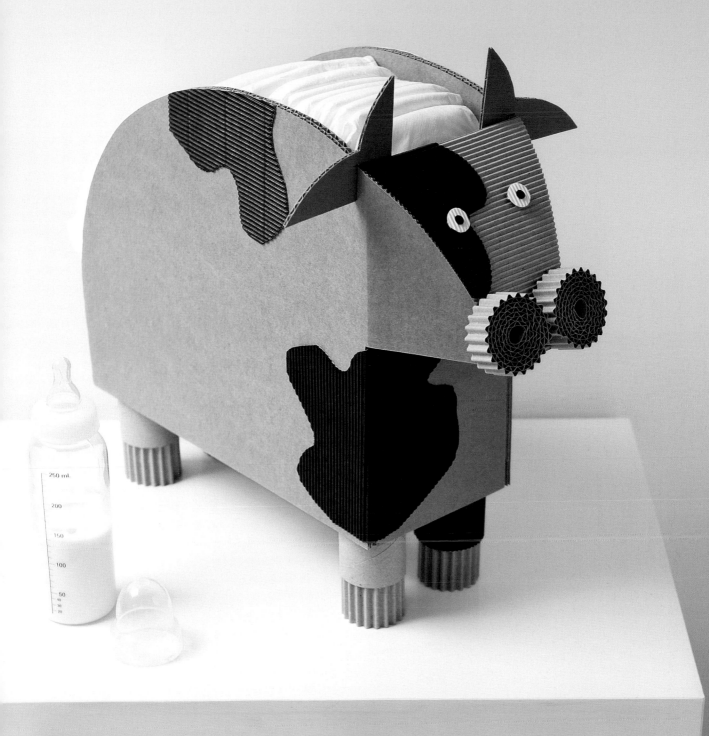
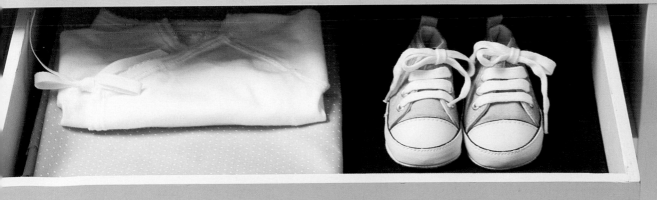

The cow (continued)

Face and tail

5
- **Draw and cut out** two ears (D) from 0.3 cardboard. Insert them into each side of the head.
- **Make** two spirals for the nostrils from two 40 x 2cm (16 x ¾in) strips of flexible cardboard. Glue them to the bottom of the head.
- **Cut out** two 1.5cm (⅝in) circles from white micro for the eyes. Glue black micro confetti to the centre of each circle for the pupils and glue the eyes in place.

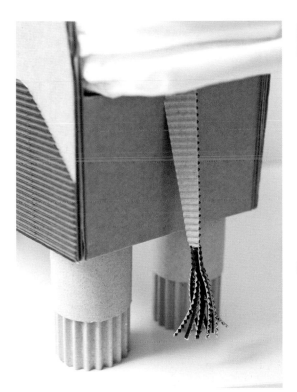

6
- **Cut out** a trapezoid (E) from kraft micro for the tail. Fold it along the dotted line.
- **Cut out** a 5cm (2in) square of black micro, create a 4cm (1¾in) fringe and glue it around the end of the tail. Make two slits in the back of the cow to slot in the tail (Diagram 3).

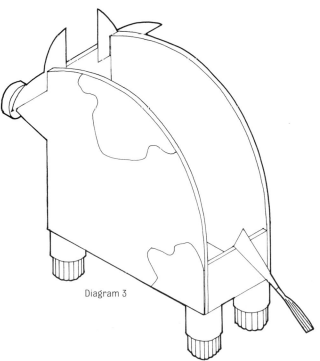

Diagram 3

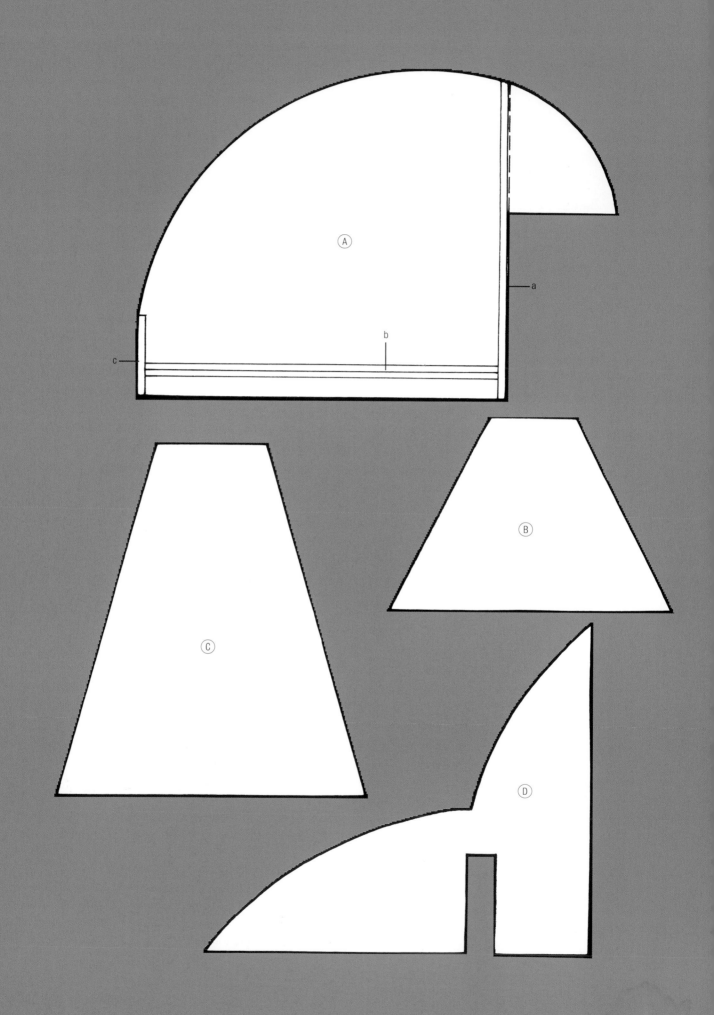

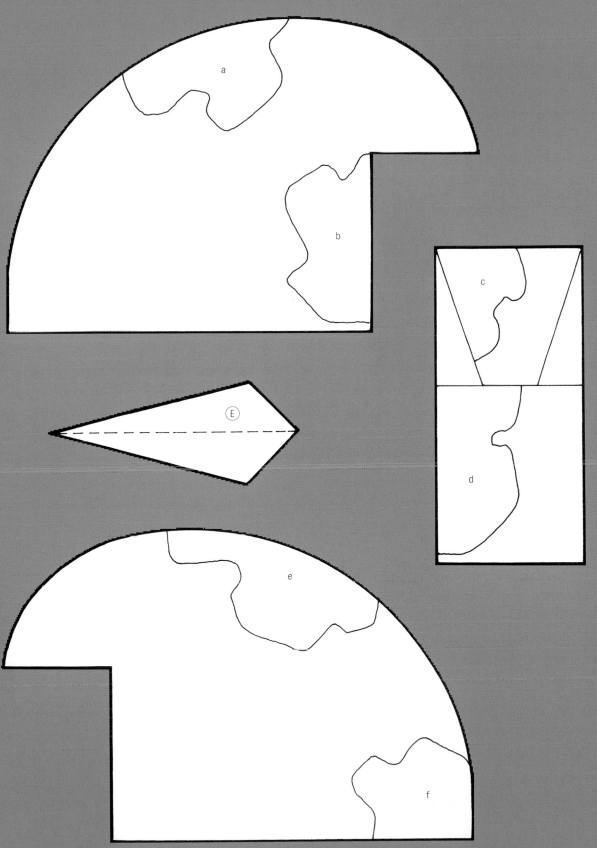

Cow – D: actual size
A, (a), (b), (c), (d), (e), (f): enlarge x 330%
B, C, E: enlarge x 150%

Body and head

1

· **Draw and cut out** two body profiles (A) from 0.6 cardboard.
· **Cut out** rectangles from 0.6 cardboard: 24 x 13cm (9¾ x 5¼in) (a) twice, and 22.5 x 13cm (8¾ x 5¼in) (b) and 13 x 11.5cm (5¼ x 4½in) (c) once. Glue the rectangles onto one of the profiles in the positions shown in (A) (Diagram 1).
· **Seal** the body together by gluing over the second body profile.

Kangaroo

Not just a light, the pouch can also store a soft toy.

SUPPLIES

· **0.6 cardboard: 1.2 x 1.2m (48 x 48in)**
· **Flexible cardboard: 30 x 30cm (12 x 12in)**
· **Kraft micro: 12 x 12cm (4¾ x 4¾in)**
· **Black micro: 5 x 5cm (2 x 2in)**
· **Two 1.5cm (⅝in) brown wooden beads**
· **Raffia**
· **Two pins with black heads**
· **Lamp base**
· **Punch**

2

· **Draw and cut out** the base of the head (B) from 0.6 cardboard.
· **Fold** the two sides of the head slightly inwards following the dotted lines (A). Glue the base between the two sides.
· **Draw and cut out** the curved part of the head (C) from flexible cardboard. Glue it to the curves of the head.

3

· **Draw and cut out** two ears (D) from kraft micro. Insert them into the slits at the top of the head and glue in position.
· **Pin and glue** the two beads in position for the eyes.
· **Draw and cut out** the nose (E) from 0.6 cardboard. Cover it with black micro and glue it onto the head.
· **Cut eight pieces** of raffia, 8cm (3¼in) in length, for the whiskers. Punch four holes on each side of the nose, thread the raffia through the holes and glue into position.

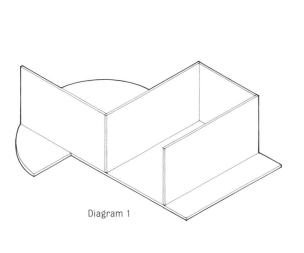

Diagram 1

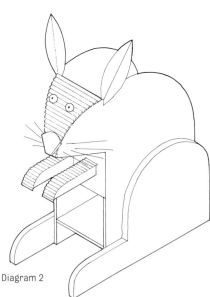

Diagram 2

The kangaroo (continued)

Legs, tail and drawer-holder

4

· **Draw and cut out** six profiles of the back leg (F). Glue together two sets of three, then glue them to each side of the body, allowing them to stick out by 2cm (¾in) at the back.

· **Draw and cut out** four front leg profiles (G). Glue two pairs together and cover the top of each pair with a strip of flexible cardboard, 3.5cm (1½in) in width.

· **Cover** the front side of the body with kraft micro and glue the front legs 3.5cm (1½in) under the head (Diagram 2).

5

· **Cut out** two triangles (H) and two 17 x 5cm (6¾ x 2in) rectangles from 0.6 cardboard for the tail. Glue the rectangles between the triangles on the sides of the right angle.

· **Cover** the inclined side of the triangle with kraft micro (Diagram 3).

· **Glue** the tail to the back of the kangaroo.

6

· **Draw and cut out** two sides (I) from 0.6 cardboard for the drawer. Cut out rectangles from 0.6 cardboard: 11 x 12cm (4¼ x 4¾in) (a) twice and 21 x 12cm (8¼ x 4¾in) (b) once.

· **Glue** the profiles onto the rectangles. Glue a rectangle of flexible cardboard to the curves of the drawer (Diagram 4).

· **Cut out** a 12 x 1cm (4¾ x ⅜in) strip of 0.6 cardboard and glue it to the start of the curve. Slide the drawer into the hollow part of the body.

7

· **Place** the lamp base inside the kangaroo.

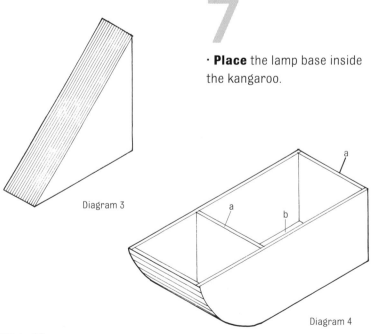

Diagram 3

Diagram 4

b

A

G

E

a

c

D

a

a

B

C

a

b

I

a

H

F

SUPPLIES

· 0.6 cardboard: 2 x 2m (80 x 80in)

· Flexible cardboard: 1 x 1m (40 x 40in)

· Black micro: 1 x 1m (40 x 40in)

· Kraft micro: 8 x 16cm (3¼ x 6¼in)

· White micro: 8 x 15 (3¼ x 6in)

· Pins

· Black paint

· Brush

Bedside table and drawer

1

· **Cut out** two 60 x 36cm (24 x 14¼in) rectangles from 0.6 cardboard for the bottom. Glue them together.

· **Cut out** six semicircles (A) of 0.6 cardboard. Glue four of these together in pairs to create the two shelves, the base and the top of the bedside table.

· **Cut out** two 19 x 13cm (7½ x 5¼in) rectangles (a), four 30 x 4cm (12 x 1¾in) strips (b) to be glued together in pairs, two 30 x 15cm (12 x 6in) rectangles (c) to be glued together, and ten 13 x 4cm (5¼ x 1¾in) strips (d) to be glued together in pairs.

· **Assemble and glue** the shelves to the strips and the bottom (Diagram 1). Space the (a) rectangles out by 17cm (6¾in) (dotted lines on A). Pin the assembly while it is drying.

Penguin

He can't fly away, so he makes the perfect bedside table!

2

· **Draw and cut out** the two sides (B) from flexible cardboard.

· **Paint** the sides black and pin in place while they dry.

· **Glue** the sides, once dry, to either side of the bedside table (Diagram 2).

· **Decorate** the top with black micro.

3

· **Draw and cut out** the base of the drawer (C) from 0.6 cardboard.

· **Cut out** three 17 x 12cm (6¾ x 4¾in) rectangles. Glue them on the straight sides of the base (Diagram 3).

· **Cut out** a 18 x 15cm (7¼ x 6in) rectangle from flexible cardboard and hollow it out in the centre with a small 6 x 2.8cm (2¼ x 1⅛in) rectangle.

· **Paint** it black. Glue it to the curved section of the drawer so that it sticks out underneath by 8mm (³⁄₈in) (Diagram 4).

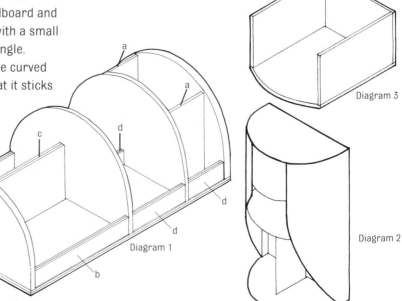

Diagram 1

Diagram 2

Diagram 3

Penguin (continued)

Beak, eyes, wings and legs

4

· **Cut out** and glue together four triangles (D) of 0.6 cardboard for the beak. Insert the beak into the inside of the drawer. Keep it inside the drawer by gluing on an 8cm (3¼in) square of kraft micro.

5

· **Cut out** two 3cm (1¼in) circles from kraft micro and two 2.5cm (1in) circles from white micro for the eyes, glue them in pairs and then together.
· **Make** two mini-spirals from black micro, glue them onto the eyes, then glue them to the drawer.

6

· **Draw and cut out** two wings (E) from black micro. Fold them along the dotted lines and glue them to the sides.

7

· **Legs:** Cut out eight 11 x 9cm (4¼ x 3¾in) rectangles from 0.6 cardboard. Glue them into two blocks of four. Cut each block at an incline of 3cm (1⅛in) (Diagram 5).

8

· **Make** a block of four 30 x 5cm (12 x 2in) rectangles. Glue the block and the legs under the table (Diagram 6).

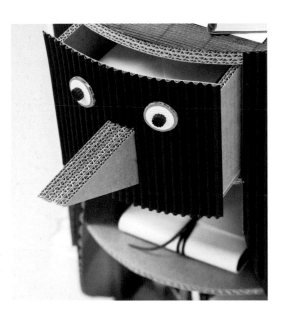

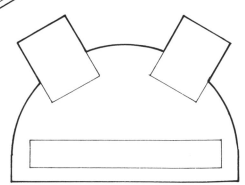

Diagram 5

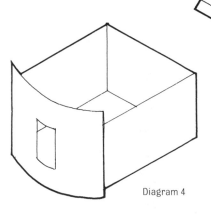

Diagram 4

Diagram 6

Penguin – templates to be enlarged x 500%, except D, which is actual size

SUPPLIES

For a doll's cradle:

· 0.6 cardboard: 2 x 2m (80 x 80in)

· Flexible cardboard: 50 x 50cm (20 x 20in)

· Black micro: 20 x 20cm (8 x 8in)

· Yellow paper: 5 x 5cm (2 x 2in)

The cradle and the head

1

· **Draw and cut out** four sides (A). Glue them together in two pairs. The whole lion is made from 0.6 cardboard.

· **Cut out** two 50 x 27cm (20 x 10¾in) rectangles for the bottom. Glue them together with the sides (Diagram 1).

· **Cut out** two 53 x 23cm (21¼ x 9¼in) rectangles (a) and glue onto the large sides. Double two 50 x 23cm (29 x 9¼in) rectangles on the large sides (Diagram 2).

· **Reinforce** the bottom with a third 50 x 26cm (20 x 10¼in) rectangle.

Lion

Always taking naps, he has a reputation as 'the lazy king'.

2

· **Draw and cut out** the head of the cradle (B) from 0.6 cardboard.

· **Draw** a 7cm (2¾in) circle in the centre of each ear. Go carefully around the outline of the circles with a cutter to remove the layer of kraft.

3

· **Nose:** Draw and cut out the nose (C) from 0.6 cardboard. Cover it in black micro and glue it onto the head in a slightly raised position.

· **Mouth:** Draw and cut out the mouth (D) from black micro. Fold along the dotted lines to give a little volume and glue in place under the nose. Glue the teeth (E) under the edge of the nose.

4

· **Eyes:** Make two spirals with 26 x 0.7cm (10¼ x ¼in) strips of flexible cardboard. Cut out two 1.5cm (⅝in) yellow circles and two 7mm (¼in) black circles and glue them to the eyes. Glue the eyes onto the head.

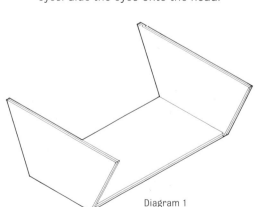

Diagram 1

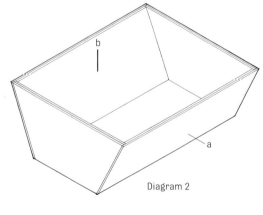

Diagram 2

The lion (continued)

Mane and legs

5
· **Cut out** a 64 x 19cm (25¼ x 7½in) rectangle of flexible cardboard for the mane.
· **Cut** 17cm (6¾in) grooves. Glue the mane in place, following the curve of the head.

6
· **Glue** the head behind (or in front of) one of the small sides of the cradle (Diagram 3).

7
· **Draw and cut out** four profiles of the front leg (F) and of the back leg (G) from 0.6 cardboard.
· **Cut out** ten triangular profiles of the front leg and of the back leg (dotted lines of the profiles). Glue them in sets of ten between each leg profile (Diagram 4).
· **Cover** the curved parts of each leg with a rectangle of flexible cardboard (Diagram 5).

8
· **Glue** the four legs onto the sides of the cradle.

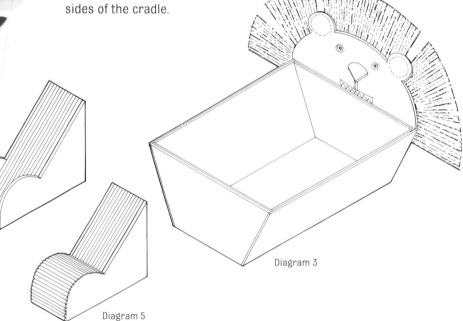

Diagram 4

Diagram 5

Diagram 3

Lion – Templates to be enlarged x 460%, except C, D, E which are actual size

SUPPLIES

· 0.6 cardboard: 2 x 2m (80 x 80in)

· Flexible cardboard: 50 x 10cm
(20 x 40in)

· Black micro: 50 x 50cm (20 x 20in)

· White micro: 40 x 10cm (16 x 4in)

· Kraft micro: 10 x 10cm (4 x 4in)

Shelf unit

1

· **Make** two square blocks as follows:

(a): Cut four 31cm (12½in) squares from 0.6 cardboard and glue together in pairs;

(b): Cut out eight rectangles with notches (A), glue them together pairs, slot them into position (Diagram 1) and glue them onto the squares from (a) (Diagram 2);

(c): Cut out six 31 x 16.4cm (12½ x 6½in) rectangles, glue four of them together in pairs, then glue one single rectangle and one double rectangle to each square from (a) (Diagram 3);

(d): Cut out eight 33.1 x 16.4cm (13¼ x 6½in) rectangles, glue them together in pairs, then glue them to the squares from (a) (Diagram 4).

Black cat

This shelf unit is as useful as it is decorative and is sure to fit right into your home.

2

· **Glue** two blocks on top of each other, with plain surfaces facing each other.

· **Decorate** the backs of the shelves with white or black micro. Leave the top two shelves undecorated.

· **Cover** the surface of the top shelves in black micro.

3

· **The drawers:** Make two boxes from 0.6 cardboard with dimensions a few millimetres smaller than the rack. These boxes must be open at the top (Diagram 5).

4

· **Cover** the exposed sides with white micro.

· **Make** handles with two spirals made from two 50 x 2cm (20 x ¾in) strips of flexible cardboard. Glue these onto each drawer.

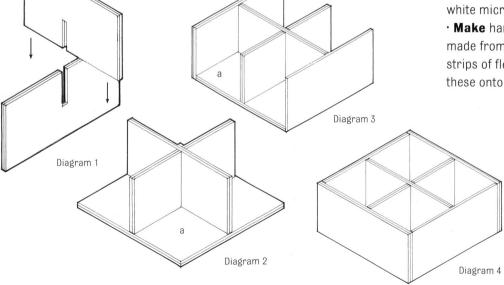

Diagram 1

Diagram 2

Diagram 3

Diagram 4

Diagram 5

Cat (continued)

Head and legs

5
· **Draw and cut out** four head silhouettes (B) from 0.6 cardboard, including two without ears.
· **Glue** the four silhouettes together (Diagram 6).
· **Cover** the head and ears with black micro.

6
· **Nose:** Draw and cut out the nose (C) from 0.6 cardboard. Cover with flexible cardboard.
· **Mouth:** Cut out three 5 x 1.2cm (2 x ½in) rectangles from kraft micro. Fold them in the middle, place them in a reversed-T position on the nose and glue them in place.
· **Whiskers:** Cut out 12 strips of 13 x 0.7cm (5¼ x ¼in) from flexible cardboard. Glue them together in pairs, then glue them in place under the nose, bending them into position.
· **Eyes:** Cut out two 3.5cm (1½in) circles from kraft micro and two 2.8cm (1¼in) circles from white micro. Glue them on top of each other. Make two mini-spirals of black micro to stick on the eyes.

7
· **Glue** the eyes to the head, slightly raising them using a small square of 0.6 cardboard.
· **Glue** the head to the back edge of the top of the shelf unit.

8
· **Legs:** draw and cut out 16 profiles (D) from 0.6 cardboard. Glue them together in four sets of four (Diagram 7).
· **Cover** one side of each leg with black micro. Glue the legs to each corner under the shelf unit.

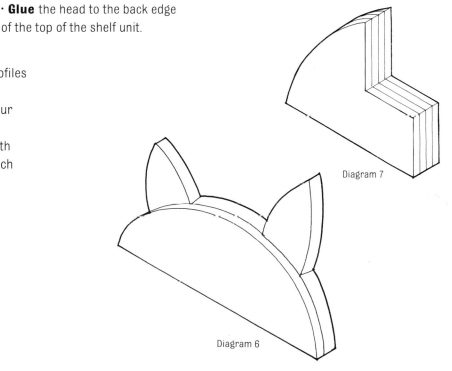

Diagram 7

Diagram 6

A DAVID & CHARLES BOOK
© Dessain et Tolra/Larousse 2009

Originally published in France as Animaux Deco en Carton

First published in the UK and USA in 2014 by F&W Media International, Ltd

David & Charles is an imprint of F&W Media International, Ltd
Brunel House, Forde Close, Newton Abbot, TQ12 4PU, UK

F&W Media International, Ltd is a subsidiary of F+W Media, Inc
10151 Carver Road, Suite #200, Blue Ash, OH 45242, USA

A catalogue record for this book is available from the British Library.

ISBN-13: 978-1-4463-0450-1 paperback
ISBN-10: 1-4463-0450-7 paperback

Printed in China by RR Donnelley for:
F&W Media International, Ltd
Brunel House, Forde Close, Newton Abbot, TQ12 4PU, UK

10 9 8 7 6 5 4 3 2 1

Management and editorial co-ordination: Colette Hanicotte
with the collaboration of Sophie Blanc and Maëva Chardin
Photographs and styling: Fabrice Besse/Sonia Roy
Proofreading: Chantal Pages assisted by Madeleine Biaujeaud
Graphic design: François Junot
Layout: Either Studio
Cover: Véronique Laporte
Production: Anne Raynaud

www.boutiqueclaudejeantet.com

F+W Media publishes high quality books on a wide range of subjects.
For more great book ideas visit: www.stitchcraftcreate.co.uk